MARKETING LANDMINES

MARKETING LANDMINES

❖

The Next Generation of Emotional Branding

KAREN TIBBALS

Karen J. Tibbals, MBA (marketing), MA (religion)
Ethical Strategist
Ethical Frames, LLC

This publication is designed to provide accurate and authoritative information in regard to the subject matter covered. It is sold with the understanding that neither the author nor the publishers are engaged in rendering legal, accounting or other professional advice. If expert assistance is desired, the services of a competent professional should be sought.

All examples cited in the book are used for illustrative purposes only; they do not constitute professional advice. All trademarks are the property of their respective companies. The publisher is not responsible for websites and their content that are not owned by the publisher.

Publisher: Ethical Frames LLC

Email: Karen@ethicalframes.com
Website: www.ethicalframes.com

ISBN: 978-1-7335749-0-7 paperback
ISBN: 978-1-7335749-1-4 ebook

The trademark for Ethical Zones™ has been applied for.

TABLE OF CONTENTS

UNDERSTANDING THE EXPLOSIVE
ENVIRONMENT

I LEFT A great job in corporate America at the end of 2011 to attend seminary and quickly ran smack into political polarization. It's not that I had been oblivious; I had been leading brand teams to understand and to market to demographic differences for a lot of years. My experience in market research, insights, and strategy meant that I had positioned products, but it was very different to *live* in the middle of this accelerated Left-Right polarization. I left suburban New Jersey (an area with expensive housing and a high cost of living) to live in a small city in the Midwest, which had almost the lowest cost housing in the country. I left a job where I worked next to highly educated people of various ethnicities from all over the world, to going to school and shopping in stores and living next to laid-off factory workers or farmers—often people who didn't have the education or politics of my former colleagues. The stores were different, the restaurants were different, and the people spoke differently. It wasn't the language; it was the culture.

The school I was enrolled in and the church I attended were in the middle of political polarization. Founded as a religious school, it had become politically Liberal, and, as a result, it had lost support from some of the Conservative founding organizations. The church was in the process of being kicked out of a larger church because they had begun welcoming LGBTQ people—more fallout from political polarization. I had gone there to study how people made decisions about applying their beliefs to the rest of their lives and I got a chance to observe it close-up in real time! I went from trying to understand people's motivations as a work project, to trying to understand people's motivations in real time in order to understand what was going on around me.

WHY THIS MATTERS TO MARKETERS

POLITICAL DIVISIVENESS HAS intensified since I left Corporate HQ market research in 2011. Brands used to try to stay out of politics. That is changing now. The increased political polarization that feels as if it is driving people apart is also affecting brands and creating marketing landmines that can bury your brand or propel it if you use it to emotionally brand. Some brands are taking a clear stand. Nike is using emotional branding in their decision to feature Colin Kaepernick in its thirtieth anniversary Just Do It ad in 2018, knowing that he would be controversial and might cause a marketing landmine. Bonobos tried to emotionally brand when they created the campaign to #EvolvetheDefinition of masculinity. It seems that Dick's Sporting Goods tried to evade the explosive power of the marketing landmine when they took a stand after the Parkland shooting to not sell guns to those under twenty-one and not sell assault rifles to anyone, but instead the marketing landmine buried them. These actions will reverberate in brand perceptions for years.

It isn't just high-profile cases that reflect this polarization. Even if brands aren't overtly taking stands, they still risk running into emotions that lead to the marketing landmines that political polarization has hidden. I'll tell you later about how Always Maxi Pads has been running a campaign for thirty years that may be alienating some potential customers—another type of marketing landmine. Coors stepped into the same trap, but when sales declined, they jumped back out.

Political polarization is reflected in the long-term change going on in the grocery store, where sales of venerable packaged goods in the center of the store are eroding. Brand powerhouses are adapting by buying companies with trendy, growing brands and then accelerating those new brands' growth with their supply chains, distribution, and marketing power. General Mills's purchase of Annie's Homegrown in 2014 has worked out well for them, with Annie's sales doubling in two years after the acquisition. Other similar transactions are the purchase of Tom's of Maine by Colgate, Ben & Jerry's ice cream by Unilever, Clorox buying Burt's Bees, and Coca-Cola buying a stake in Honest Tea and buying Fuze, Odwalla, and Vitamin Water. But these acquisitions don't always work. Campbell's purchases of Bolthouse Foods and Garden Fresh

Gourmet were supposed to do the same trick but didn't, so Campbell's is now selling them to raise cash.

While packaged goods companies are buying "hot" new products, they are selling underperforming older brands to other firms who think they know how to revive them. For example, in 2018, Smucker's sold the Pillsbury baking line, Hungry Jack pancakes, and Martha White baking mixes to Brynwood Partners. Brynwood had already bought brands such as SunnyD and Juicy Juice from Procter & Gamble and Nestle (respectively). Smucker's is keeping the Folgers coffee line, another brand that Procter & Gamble jettisoned, but they are attempting to position it as a more premium brand. In the effort to refresh their portfolio, they are ignoring the underlying power of the brands they have, power that could be unleashed by using the next generation of emotional branding.

HOW THIS BOOK CAN HELP

WHAT I DISCOVERED in my time at seminary was that research can help a brand navigate the emotional minefield of political polarization. I uncovered academic research results that can help to create a deeper understanding of where the marketing landmines are planted as a result of political polarization. Using these insights can help you hear what your customers say in a new way, making your focus groups more powerful, so you're more likely to find the marketing landmines before you trigger them. These insights can also add a powerful layer to any segmentation research and targeting you do. Finally, you can employ these techniques to create messages that take advantage of the power behind the marketing landmines to emotionally brand for your product.

Marketing is already making use of behavioral economics and emotional research. This book represents the next advance in marketing by demonstrating how advertising can utilize another set of academic research findings from recent anthropological, psychological, and political science. Here, I explain the theories to give you a grounding and use examples from politics, culture, and advertising to make the theories relevant.

Although these theories are relatively newly described, they describe timeless truths that have already been utilized by marketing professionals. These theories have become even more relevant because of the increasing polarization of the country. Prior to this political division, it was much easier to operate, and brands could remain neutral. Now, marketing landmines are hidden in plain sight and may hit you unaware. Knowing these theories will help you maneuver around the triggers that are buried everywhere.

As I mentioned, this book arose out of my own personal journey. I had had a wonderful three-decade-long career in insights that I loved, because I had a passion for understanding why people act the way they do. But I had a burning personal question: How do people apply their religious faith to their business lives? I finally left my market research position to go to seminary to study this. (Note: this was a seminary on the progressive left of the church, very different from what most people think of when they think of religion.)

I realize that it is odd to include religion in a book about marketing and advertising, but I am because what I found shocked me: Although people believed it was their faith that drove their decisions, it wasn't. Instead, it was a *morality* based on their psychology that was disguised as religion. One clue was something that my Old Testament professor said: The Bible can be used to justify whatever position you want. You can find a passage to back up whatever you want.

I include this comment because, when we listen to our target audience and they mention religion, marketers may tune out and not realize where it is coming from. Most of what people talk about in religious terms can be understood as psychology—that is what I will focus on in this book. Please don't be scared that I am trying to convert you; I am not! I am trying to describe what is going on, and religion is a part of it that shouldn't be ignored. But you need to hear the research with a new set of ears and a new set of glasses to really understand what is going on. I call that set of glasses Ethical Frames.

I came back to market research and marketing after my sojourn in the religious world because I thought this insight was so revolutionary that marketers like yourself needed to understand what I had learned.

ETHICAL ZONES–HARD TO SEE AND UNDERSTAND

THE INSIGHT I am describing here is invisible to us until we look at it in a new way. Just like fish not being aware that they are in water, or people not being aware that they are breathing oxygen, we aren't aware of our Ethical Zones™. They matter a lot—so much so that some people are willing to die for them. Despite our strong commitment to these ideas, we don't think about them, we just react. It's only when we run into people who have different beliefs that we start to see that differences exist. But rather than appreciate what others bring, we judge others for having different beliefs. We call them prejudiced and unethical, without trying to understand. When we don't understand the context that these beliefs arise out of and what the beneficial parts of their belief system are, then we aren't being fair. Reading this book will open your eyes and bring you to a new level of understanding.

When I started talking to people about these issues, I heard the suggestion people should learn moral reasoning. After all, if everybody just thought deeply about the ethical decisions, they would agree, right? (As if!) Similarly, ethics classes are supposed to teach moral reasoning and that will make our society more ethical, right? However, no one has demonstrated that ethics classes change anything. In fact, I recently overheard a discussion between two ethics professors, one from a libertarian perspective and one progressive, that demonstrated that ethics are basically used to support our ingoing beliefs. There has even been a set of studies that compared ethics professors to other professors that concluded that ethics professors aren't any more ethical than others. (Note: To read this for yourself, check out Cheeseburger Morality at https://aeon.co/essays/how-often-do-ethics-professors-call-their-mothers.) If knowing ethics doesn't help ethics professors become more ethical, then, it seems, it doesn't help to learn moral reasoning.

Why does this happen? Two reasons. One is that we humans pick and choose ideas and facts that support our pre-existing beliefs, which is called "motivated reasoning." Thus, we never really consider and engage with ideas that challenge our beliefs. Second, ethical judgments are made instantaneously. There is a debate about whether people ever think those decisions through. Some say that moral responses are instinctual because they happen so quickly. Others claim that most decisions reflect decisions that had been thought through at an earlier point in time and they are made so fast because they aren't rethought every time.

Regardless of which explanation is true, there is consensus that people don't rethink their ethical decisions every time a situation comes up; they respond the way they responded the time before that, whether it is instinct or something else.

HOW TO READ THIS BOOK

THIS BOOK DRAWS on several academic theories. It leans heavily on Jonathan Haidt's Moral Foundations theory but also uses Alan Fiske's Relational Models theory, Steven Pinker's views on rationality, and Spiral Dynamics developed by Clare Graves. I find the Spiral Dynamics theory a helpful addition because it describes the reactions of fear and disdain that people have toward those who have different dominant Ethical Zones and because it adds another Ethical Zone. But I don't tell you these theories. I apply them to real-world marketing and advertising examples.

As you read this book, try to withhold the judgment you would normally make. You might be tempted to take this as an opportunity to get angry about those with whom you disagree and try to come up with arguments to convince people that your way is right. But the research shows that those types of arguments backfire. When you argue that way, your opponent actually becomes more entrenched in their opinions—the arguments themselves act as a trigger. The other side already knows basically what you think.

Instead, try to approach this discussion as if you were an anthropologist studying the culture. Look for the truths behind the ideas that don't agree with your pre-existing ideas. When we allow for the truth behind two conflicting ideas to emerge, it can lead us to a greater truth. In market research, we called it synthesis. Others call it paradox. In seminary, we called this thinking "both/and." The idea is that there can be truth in two different ideas, and if that is true, then resolving the conflict can lead to a greater insight. Look for the glimpses of truth. Remember, as Spiral Dynamics states, if your reactions are fear or disdain, that is a clue you are looking at a different dominant Ethical Zone. This is the key to achieving the next Ethical Zone: Understanding.

Use this also as an opportunity to understand yourself better as well as those you are reading about. Self-awareness will be helpful as you walk this path.

This is difficult work. It involves challenging some of your strongly held beliefs. It requires that you go beyond your normal motivated reasoning (everyone has this!). We need to approach this effort with humility. The world is a complicated place and there are unexpected consequences to our actions. We may think we know the "right" thing to do, but what if we are wrong? What if what we think is right actually makes things worse? Unintended consequences are real. The Wikipedia entry for unintended consequences includes the cobra effect. This refers to a time when the British government in India offered a bounty for cobra corpses, leading to people breeding cobras. When the cobras were set free after the bounty ended, the country experienced an increase in cobras.

Hold on to your beliefs lightly.

THE BOOK'S STRUCTURE

THE STRUCTURE OF this book is as follows: The next five chapters describe the five Moral Foundations as first described by Jonathan Haidt (a professor at NYU, author of the book *The Righteous Mind*), illustrated with examples from culture, advertising, and product usage. I start with the Ethical Zone (my term for the Moral Foundations) of Belonging and Community because it influences all the rest. The next four chapters discuss Respect for Authority, Sacredness, Fairness, and Care/Harm. Each chapter will talk about what the origin of the Ethical Zone is, how it varies by Conservative versus Liberal, the psychological and neurological underpinnings of it, how it has been used in marketing, and give examples of where each has buried landmines.

Those chapters are followed by a chapter on Rationality and Reason, which adds a new Zone, drawing from UCLA anthropologist Alan Fiske's Relational Models theory and some thoughts from Harvard University professor Steven Pinker. This completes the basic Ethical Zones model. Here's a preview of the model:

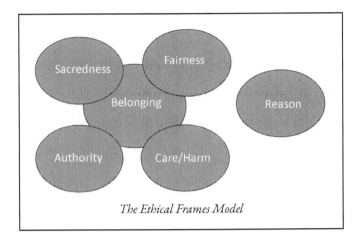

The Ethical Frames Model

After I have reviewed the basics of the six Ethical Zones, there is a chapter using cultural conflicts to illustrate how they result from different interpretations and importance given to the various Ethical Zones. Then, three chapters focus on the armies that planted the marketing landmines: Conservatives and Liberals, including descriptions that can be used to start building a target audience profile for your marketing plan. Next, I go more deeply into the basis behind political polarization, both biological and psychological. After that is the market research chapter—how to map the marketing landmines that affect your category and brand.

The book continues with two chapters on how you can use these theories to change the battlefield and use the Ethical Frames model to reach the next level of emotional branding. Don't skip the final three chapters, Planning for the Negotiation, a cautionary chapter on the Rules of Engagement, and Reviewing the Plan. And there is an Afterword about a new controversial campaign that was launched after the book was written that brings up some slightly different issues.

Because this is difficult work, it may be too difficult to do alone. That's why I offer workshops that enable you to understand this theory on a deep level and help you develop concrete ways to apply this model to your own situation. For more details, check out my website, www.ethicalframes.com.

I hope this book helps you more deeply understand what drives people's emotions, thoughts, and actions and that you can apply this information in emotional branding of your product, segmenting your target audience, and making use of the power behind the marketing landmines.

CHAPTER 1

WHICH SIDE ARE YOU ON? BELONGING AND COMMUNITY

H OW WE FEEL about the group we belong to is one of the most powerful forces in the world—one that marketers ignore. We pretend that our customers are individuals and are blind to the effect of the groups that they belong to.

Jonathan Haidt recognized the power of Belonging as one of the five areas in his book *The Righteous Mind*. He uses the term *Moral Foundations* to describe the five areas but I call them Ethical Zones because I feel it is more useful. (I add a sixth later which I will explain in more detail when we get there.) Here's a graphic description of the model I am building in this book, with the first Ethical Zone, Belonging, highlighted.

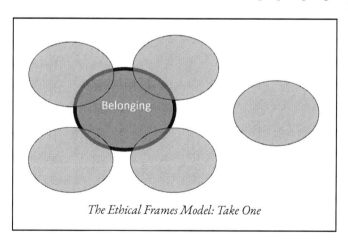

The Ethical Frames Model: Take One

THE GOOD SIDE OF BELONGING

MY BOOK STARTS with Belonging and Community (which Haidt calls loyalty) because the group you belong to drives *everything*; all the other factors I will describe depend on which community you belong to. I like the words *Belonging and Community* better than the word *loyalty* because it doesn't have the same negative connotations. Part of my feelings about this Ethical Zone arises out of the importance my religious denomination places on Community support.

Community is an incredibly powerful force. It is so powerful that people with strong social connections have been shown to live longer lives. Lack of Community is considered to be a contributing factor to what are now called deaths of despair—addiction and suicide. Belonging is so crucial that it affects individual self-esteem. Research shows that those who strongly identify with a group find their identity in that group, and when the group "loses," their self-esteem plummets.

THE DOWNSIDE OF BELONGING

THE EFFECTS OF Belonging and Community are not all good; those who do not belong to our group are the out-group. This results in "othering": regarding those who aren't part of our group as less worthy, or less deserving, or even less human. Winning over the out-group becomes important. And winning leads to a burst of dopamine, the hormone that gives us pleasure.

The Belonging effect is so dominant that people will make errors if the group around them makes errors; accuracy doesn't matter. For example, people misidentify colors or line length when the people around them give erroneous information and switch their position on an issue if they are told that their group feels a different way. It doesn't even have to be a group that you have strong ties to; even an insignificant group membership can have this effect. This is probably a contributing factor to people believing "fake news."

BELONGING: AN INCREDIBLY POWERFUL FORCE

THE BELONGING AND Community factor has an evolutionary origin. Groups that had higher group participation were more likely to survive; thus, we humans are all descended from people who knew how to cooperate. Belonging is an instinctual drive.

Young children develop a strong sense of Belonging very early in life, before they are verbal. Evidence for this includes the fact that young children spend more time looking at people who look similar to them, and that their mirror neurons light up when someone who is like them is pricked by a needle but don't when the person is an "other." In describing this strong effect, political scientist Lilliana Mason of the University of Maryland writes that all humans have a deeply rooted in-group bias.

This unconscious reaction that children exhibit continues into adulthood. Literally, our brains work differently for in-group members versus out-group members. Adults' saliva secretions vary also when an in-group member is sad versus an out-group member and their neurons react differently based on the social category of the face they see. These reactions happen fast—within 300 milliseconds! Those with stronger ties to an in-group (more likely Conservatives) use similar portions of the brain for both the group and themselves; those with less strong ties don't. People have similar brain responses to being sad themselves as when they see people in their in-group being sad, but not when the person is from the out-group. People who sweat more when they see pictures of those in an out-group are more likely to discriminate against them. These physiological reactions probably explain the research results that demonstrate that the vast majority of us have what is called "implicit bias."

Some of the displays of Belonging that we see today are in allegiance to sports teams and in the intense bonds that are formed among army buddies. Thinking about sports and war brings in another important aspect of Belongingness: winning. What is important to those in a group is that the group wins. Winning drives an even greater sense of cohesion.

BELONGING BONDS ARE LOOSENING

THE BELONGING BONDS in society have been loosening recently. Research shows that Americans are the most independent of any country's people and are becoming more isolated and independent. In his book *Bowling Alone*, Robert Putnam documents a decline in civic participation in institutions, churches, and neighborhood communities. Americans have lost trust in their institutions. Further, there has been an increase in social sorting—people are more likely to live with others just like them and marry people just like them. So instead of sharing a community with people of different backgrounds and different beliefs, getting to know them, and giving them the benefit of the doubt, we have fewer broad community ties.

There are variations in the degree to which these social Belonging bonds have loosened. Those who moved less (such as those who stayed in rural areas) have higher levels of Belonging than those who moved away. Those who stayed in the place they were born tend to be higher in Belonging to a physical community and tend to be Conservative in their outlook. They have stronger participation in group activities. Liberals have moved away, loosening their ties. That doesn't mean Liberals don't have a sense of a group that they belong to, it's just different and not (as much) the place they are from.

A clear manifestation of this difference between loosening of place-based identification is found in nationalism attitudes. Liberals are citizens of the world, while Conservatives are citizens of the place they live in and country they belong to. It's not surprising that brands such as Walmart, Budweiser, and Remington that appeal to Conservatives are more likely to use patriotic imagery. A GMC pickup truck with an American flag image superimposed over the GMC logo is probably driven by a Conservative. The Super Bowl Budweiser ad with the Clydesdales that was done as a tribute to commemorate an anniversary of 9/11 probably appeals more to Conservatives.

POLITICAL PARTIES ARE THE NEW WAY TO BELONG

DESPITE THE DIFFERENCE in nationalism, both Liberals and Conservatives have a sense of Belonging to their political party. Lilliana Mason suggests that the factors of social sorting, independence, and isolation, together with social media, are responsible for the increasing degree to which people rely on their political identity for their sense of Belonging. Social media is one factor driving us apart and causing some of us to substitute online interaction for in-person interaction.

Humans desire connection so deeply that we use any way we can to try to satisfy that need, even if that way isn't effective at satisfying that need. In fact, research demonstrates that social media have the opposite effect of in-person contacts, with a negative effect on psychological well-being, including an increase in depression. There is now a beginning of an awareness that social media can't substitute for what some call the "meat world" or IRL (in real life).

Those same media choices that substitute for in-person interaction are also contributing to an increase of alignment of worldview with political view. There used to be conservative Democrats and liberal Republicans, but that is disappearing. Political parties are our new teams, our new way to belong. This is the new tribalism.

MARKETING IMPLICATIONS

MARKETERS HAVE HARNESSED the power of Belonging in loyalty programs, a group that you belong to with a "loose connection". Marketing efforts that create communities such as online forums for people with conditions and diseases such as hives or COPD are another way that marketers have been mining the power of Community for a brand.

But the marketing implications of this theory go beyond this. The world has become binary. Winning becomes more important than anything else. Companies that take a stand on an issue that Liberals care about, like Nike, are sending a signal that it is siding with Liberals. Conversely, siding with Conservatives sends a signal that the product is for

Conservatives and *not* for Liberals. This is one element of emotional branding.

Because of this increased polarization, brand strategies that worked years ago may not work today.

An analysis of MRI data from a twenty-five-year period shows a consistent pattern of Liberals and Conservatives using different products. Conservatives buy more Jif peanut butter, Wranglers and Dockers clothing, Cool Whip topping, Tyson chicken, and Betty Crocker cake mixes. Liberals eat more Ben & Jerry's ice cream and drink more Celestial Seasonings tea, Poland Spring water, Sam Adams and Corona Extra beer.

Thus, the change in trends of packaged foods described in the introduction is a direct result of the increased political polarization.

Liberals prefer a "sharper" and more distinct taste profile than Conservatives: Liberals eat arugula and kale; Conservatives eat iceberg lettuce. The fact that President George H.W. Bush didn't like broccoli fits perfectly with the taste profile preferred by Conservatives. Conservatives drink light beer; Liberals, IPAs (India pale ales).

Liberals are more likely to be vegetarian. Conservatives are more likely to eat at both fast-food and other chain restaurants such as Arby's, Applebee's, Cracker Barrel, and Burger King. Liberals don't (at least as much.) Patronizing national brands and chain restaurants conveys that you belong to the Conservative tribe. Not using national brands and instead following the latest trends are signals that you belong to the Liberal tribe. That's why there were so many chain restaurants where I went to school in the Midwest. When a new ethnic restaurant opened, the college would rally around to try to support it. Unfortunately, there weren't enough Liberals to support these new ethnic restaurants, and the Conservatives wouldn't consider them, so the restaurants would close.

Another signal of Belonging is the media you consume. Fox News is an obvious choice for Conservatives; MSNBC is the choice of Liberals. When USAA the insurance and finance company decided to exit advertising on Fox News's *Hannity* show in order to avoid opinion-based news programs, they faced pushback from its core customer base of veterans and military families (probably Conservatives), so they reversed the decision. As I finish writing this, advertisers have abandoned Tucker Carlson's show because of his comment that immigrants are dirtier.

Media buying in this tribal world has planted marketing landmines that can be triggered without warning.

There are differences in which TV shows people watch and how they use social media. Liberals watch shows like *Black-ish*, *Broad City*, *The Good Place*, and *Will and Grace*. Conservatives (mostly) watch very different shows. They are more likely to watch shows such as *The Brave*, *Blue Bloods*, *Lethal Weapon*, *NCIS*, as well as reality-based shows like *The Apprentice* and *Shark Tank*. *Dancing with the Stars* and *Star Trek* are some of the few shows that both groups watch.

When brands focus on Liberal issues and the latest trends, they are ignoring the third of the country that doesn't feel that way. (They may also be ignoring the needs of the ethnic groups who align with Liberals politically but have Conservative attitudes.) But this happens both because of the skew of those who work in marketing (college educated) and because marketing research tends to be done in major metros, where there are fewer Conservatives.

The words that Liberals and Conservatives use about the feeling of Belonging are different and reflect the different emphasis. Conservatives might use words with a positive connotation such as *loyalty*, *patriot*, and *homeland*, and negative words such as *deserter*, *deceiver*, *foreign*, and *betrayal*. Liberal words for this zone might include *communal*, *group*, and *solidarity*. Both use words like *treason* and *treacherous*. To Liberals, the words *foreign* and *immigrant* are not negative, but to Conservatives they are. This means that when you work on emotionally branding, the words that signal Belonging need to be chosen carefully.

Advertising can touch on the Ethical Zone of Belonging and Community in many ways. Just by saying that other people in your group buy this product is one simple way. But it doesn't have to be that direct.

UNDERSTANDING THE POWER OF MARKETING LANDMINES

IN 2018, NIKE tried to make the power of Belonging work for them. They jumped into a pre-existing conflict with both feet by using Colin Kaepernick as the face of the thirtieth anniversary Just Do It campaign. Two years earlier, Kaepernick started trying to draw attention to the killings of unarmed black men by kneeling during the national anthem instead of standing at attention. A year later, he was out of a job and had sued the NFL for colluding in not hiring him. Other athletes began imitating him, leading the NFL to institute a policy requiring athletes to stand during the national anthem.

President Donald J. Trump weighed in by scolding players for disrespecting the flag. Conservatives definitely see it as a patriotism issue, with half of Trump supporters saying they would boycott NFL games over the protest; on the other hand, Liberals are cheering for the attention being paid to an issue they feel needs that attention. The NFL ban didn't stand very long; they reversed themselves after the controversy erupted. The NFL was caught between Conservatives, who are more likely to watch televised sports, and the Liberals. There were high emotions on both sides.

So, when Nike decided to jump into this emotionally charged issue, they had to know they were walking into a marketing landmine. Their brand had been lagging in perceptions among younger consumers (who are more likely to be Liberal) and among ethnic consumers. The emotional power of the landmine helped Nike to signal that they were on the side of those Liberal and ethnic customers. It didn't matter much to Nike that white Conservatives set their shoes on fire and threatened to boycott the company; those people weren't their intended target audience.

As I write this in November 2018, the results of the last two months have been mixed; Nike's stock price dropped even though sales were up substantially. It remains to be seen what the long-term results will be, but Nike has certainly begun to emotionally brand their product line, even as they exploded a marketing landmine.

Unlike Nike, Dick's Sporting Goods tried to avoid the emotional power of a highly charged issue when they announced that they would no longer sell assault rifles and would restrict sales of guns to those over twenty-one after the Parkland shooting in February 2018. Dick's tried to soften the impact on Conservatives by including a line in their press release about supporting the Second Amendment. Further, in interviews, the CEO went on TV shows to say that he is a gun owner himself. They were relying on facts, on reason and rationality.

But when it was discovered that Dick's had contributed money to a gun-control lobbyist, there was a backlash. The NRA came out against

Dick's, and some major gun manufacturers decided to not sell guns to Dick's. Why did the NRA and its supporters have this extreme reaction? I have been struggling with this question as I have been working on this book, but I am Liberal, so it's not surprising that I don't understand. I finally found a clue in the book *Braving the Wilderness* by Brené Brown. Because she grew up in gun culture, she understands that culture in a way I can't.

Brown explained that it isn't necessarily the guns themselves; it is what the guns represent to that group. Guns have come to be part of what it means to be an American, so if you are Conservative, that's the Belonging and Community Ethical Zone. Without quite realizing what was happening, even though they are embedded in the gun culture, Dick's was stepping into a Belonging and Community marketing landmine, and it exploded, despite their best efforts.

How has this affected Dick's? Since then, Dick's retail sales are off, even though the stock price has climbed in the six months since the announcement. The real test will be long-term sales, so it remains to be seen. (I'll revisit Dick's in later chapters as I explain where another landmine exploded.)

Delta Airlines also got caught in blowback of explosion and their landmine may also have had an impact on where Amazon put their second headquarters. After the Parkland shooting, Delta eliminated a discount they had been providing to NRA members. The pro-gun members of the Georgia state legislature punished Delta for this by eliminating a fuel-tax exemption that would have saved Delta millions of dollars. This move didn't just affect Delta; other airlines who fly out of the Atlanta hub lost their exemption as well.

While this action by the Georgia state legislature could be perceived as being self-serving and rational (Georgia gets more money if they eliminate the exemption), the legislature was warned that the action could negatively affect perceptions of Georgia as a business-friendly state. The Ethical Zone of Belonging is such a strong force that they didn't heed that warning. Interestingly, it may also have had an impact on Amazon's choice of HQ2. Atlanta had been in the running for the Amazon HQ2, but Amazon didn't choose Atlanta, and instead decided to split their HQ2 into two cities: Long Island City in Queens, New York, and Crystal City, Virginia. Did the state legislature decision about Delta impact the Amazon decision? We may never know, but it could have.

Levi's is approaching the marketing landmine of gun control in the same way that Nike approached the NFL issue. Levi's wants to make themselves more attractive to younger consumers, so they are using the issue of gun control to emotionally brand. Interestingly, they think they are being inclusive and appear not to realize that those who had a problem with Dick's would have the same problem with them. Because their target is younger consumers, it won't matter.

In their 2018 campaign #EvolvetheDefinition, Bonobos (a young, trendy company that sells men's pants, which was bought by Walmart in 2017) tried to start a conversation about masculinity, challenging the traditional definition. In a ninety-second documentary-style video, they had a variety of men read definitions of masculinity and then explain the problems with the definition, finally making suggestions on how they would make it more inclusive. (You can see the video for yourself at https://www.youtube.com/watch?v=j6jz2Jma5-s.) The men included gays and trans men, including one who says, "that doesn't sound like me." That video (which was posted on social media and on YouTube) got lots and lots of comments, about twice as many negative as positive. One commenter started with this: "This is garbage. Men need to act like men and not women."

So, who are the people who are reacting so negatively? Of course, these negative reactions are coming from men who are Conservative. The reaction by Conservatives highlights another key part of Belonging: your gender. Gender is one of the first ideas you learn as a child, about which subtribe you belong to: male or female. Thus, it's not surprising that challenging the definition of masculinity (read: challenging the Belonging that Conservative men feel) created a storm among those who think the definition of masculinity is just fine the way it is. And recent research seems to indicate that men who feel insecure about their masculinity may be the most likely to defend it in a politically charged way—exactly the way that men responded to the Bonobos campaign.

Of course, Liberals will disagree, which is another level of why this is in the Belonging and Community Ethical Zone and sets up a marketing landmine on the other side. In fact, Liberals are championing this issue, taking it even further, seeing it as a crucial part of making the world a safer place for gays and trans people. An example of this Liberal movement is a panel discussion at Cannes in 2018 entitled "The Future of Masculinity" by Faith Popcorn's Brain Reserve, which included a zine. The website for the zine states that it is "exploring how masculinity is evolving." Brain Reserve's remit is to focus on future trends, which they read from Liberals, ignoring the Conservatives.

Importantly, among its target audience of young trendy men, Bonobos succeeded in emotional branding, and the marketing landmine it set off among Conservatives doesn't really matter, unless it matters to its owner, Walmart.

In the next chapter, I will discuss how another Ethical Zone (Respect for Authority) contributed another powerful emotion that helped make these marketing landmines even more explosive.

As we will discuss in later chapters, Belonging interacts with the other zones. Those who belong to the same group are more likely to be viewed as Sacred, more likely to deserve more, more likely to be cared about, and more likely to be respected as leaders and authority figures. Because President Obama is biracial, he didn't belong to the white in-group, and thus was less likely to be respected as a legitimate president by Conservatives, who have stronger in-group identification.

CULTURAL DIFFERENCES

A LIMITATION OF this book is that it is focused on the dominant culture in the US. Most of what is included doesn't apply to the various ethnic groups in the US, such as blacks, Latinos, Asians, and Muslims. Unlike whites in the US, these groups haven't undergone the shift to have their politics align with their underlying Ethical Zones. Although these ethnic groups may *politically* align with Liberals, they themselves are not Liberal in many of their attitudes. The Saturday Night Live *Black Jeopardy* sketch, which appeared right before the 2016 election, captured this dynamic by highlighting how similar experiences and attitudes are between the white working class and blacks, despite the prejudice whites feel against blacks as an out-group.

Because ethnic groups are out-groups, and thus are a target for Conservatives in their attempt to increase Belonging, the politics of ethnic groups is more clearly what is called "identity politics." Identity politics occurs when your ethnicity itself drives your political views. Thus, the emotional branding that Nike used in the Colin Kaepernick campaign has two different forces behind it: identity politics for nondominant ethnic groups and the emotional power of the Ethical Zone of Belonging for both white Liberals and white Conservatives.

A further caveat: Americans (and people from other developed countries) have very different viewpoints than those of people from less developed countries. The researchers who documented this skew have called the developed world phenomenon WEIRD: Western, educated, industrialized, rich, and democratic. Americans are WEIRD, so are Western Europeans and Australians. Since much psychological research is conducted among college students from WEIRD countries, the results are not necessarily representative of people from relatively less developed countries nor representative of those who are Conservative. Thus, you need to think about whether psychological research applies beyond the WEIRD countries.

Among the few bits of research that have been done outside of the WEIRD areas, it is clear that more recently developed cultures have higher levels of the Ethical Zone of Belonging than the West. This is reflected in an Eastern European saying: "If you're in a position of power and you don't use it to enrich yourself, you're stealing from your family." (Credit to Brad Agle of Brigham Young University for turning me on to the saying.)

A story from Africa illustrates this point. Over a century ago, missionaries from the US started a hospital in western Africa. For decades, the administration of the hospital came from the organizers in the developed world. Eventually, the board decided to transition the hospital to local control. The new administrator (a local) embezzled some money. The board of directors thought that they had just made a bad choice, so they fired that person and hired a different local person as administrator. That person embezzled too!

After reading Jonathan Haidt's book *The Righteous Mind*, the board figured out what was going on. That African country was extremely high in the Belonging and Community Ethical Zone. When an African was asked for money by a family member or a community member, they had to say yes. Their Ethical Zone of Belonging was stronger than any responsibility they felt to the hospital, the patients, or the donors. A study of African countries using the Spiral Dynamics system has documented this high level of Belonging, although it used different terminology.

CONSOLIDATING WHAT WE HAVE LEARNED

THE BELONGING AND Community Ethical Zone is the fundamental building block to understand why the political landscape is so fractured and why it sets up an emotional minefield. Belonging arises out of our evolutionary history and affects our brain functioning, saliva production, and sweat. It is a powerful force that affects our opinions, our self-image, and even our longevity. The degree to which people belong to groups varies by political affiliation and the decline of other affiliations has led to political affiliation becoming the dominant way of Belonging.

Belonging has both a good side and a bad side. The good side is increased life span. The dark side of Belonging is the degree to which we think of people not like us as "other." Your "group" winning has become extremely important and that leads to people avoiding things that are favored by other groups. This affects brand usage. The Ethical Zone of Belonging is stronger in non-Western countries and among Conservatives.

CHAPTER 2

WHO DO YOU FOLLOW? AUTHORITY AND LEADERSHIP

IF YOU ARE wondering what Authority has to do with advertising, you might be tempted to skip this chapter. Before you do, read this one paragraph. If you are building a brand, you need to know how your target audience feels about Authority to fully understand their feelings toward your brand. Feelings about Authority affect new product adoption and the life cycle of a brand. They also affect who might be an appropriate spokesperson, brand image and media choices. So this very important concept underlies emotional branding.

Here's the Ethical Frames model with the second Ethical Zone named:

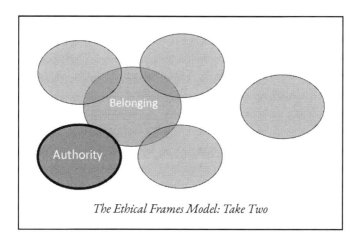

The Ethical Frames Model: Take Two

Just like Belonging and Community, Respect for Authority comes out of our evolutionary history. Groups that had good leaders survived; thus, we are all descended from them. Alan Fiske (the anthropologist who originated the Relational Model theory, an input into Moral Foundations theory) concluded that as societies increased in size and density, they went from communal sharing to having an authority figure who helped them organize more effectively. Then, as the population continued to increase, Respect for Authority became more important in determining what is viewed as right and wrong.

Respect for Authority is also noted as a stage of Western childhood psychological development. In that stage, young children believe that "right" is what an authority figure said. After puberty, this research found that children age out of unquestioning acceptance of what an authority figure says.

But that research with children came out of a well-educated Western-world sensibility (as mentioned earlier—the WEIRD societies, Western educated industrial rich democracies), so that paradigm isn't true for people in smaller and less densely populated societies and other cultures. Just like in the other Ethical Zones, there are differences within the population, both by group and individually. In the US, Conservatives tend to be higher on Respect for Authority.

THE PSYCHOLOGICAL UNDERPINNINGS OF AUTHORITY

IN THE PREVIOUS chapter, I talked about how all humans need to Belong, that we all need Community, and that politics has become the dominant group identification, and I talked about some of the differences between Liberals and Conservatives. But what determines how you feel about Authority?

Political science and psychological research offer several potential explanations. One relevant area of research says people differ in their need to come to a quick conclusion, (called High Need for Cognitive Closure or HNFCC) and that this is what drives political affiliation. People who have HNFCC tend to be Conservative and have high Respect for Authority. (Note that this has no association with intelligence! They aren't stupid, they just need to come to conclusions quickly.)

Another way to clearly identify people who are high in Authority is to ask questions about parenting style originally created by Stanley Feldman and used extensively in research by Hetherington and Weiler. The questions all start like this: "Which one is more important for a child to have?" Questions are asked in four areas:

1. Independence versus respect for elders
2. Obedience versus self-reliance
3. Curiosity versus good manners
4. Being considerate versus being well-behaved

Those who answer respect, obedience, good manners, and being well-behaved are more likely to have what Hetherington calls a "fixed" mind set, which indicates a Conservative mind set and one that is high in Respect for Authority. This mind set comes from their worldview. Those who believe the world is a scary place choose obedience-related attributes, and those who think the world is a relatively safe place choose openness-related attributes. Thus, a fixed mind set and parenting style is one way respect for Authority is transmitted to the next generation. Importantly, these differences also relate to personality differences: Those who are high in Authority tend to be low on openness to new experiences and high on conscientiousness, two of the big five personality traits.

Thus, being high in Authority is associated with maintaining order and control, as well as with obedience and fending off chaos. When you have an authority figure in charge, you know what to expect. Implicit in this is a responsibility that the leader has for his followers. Further, there is consistency and structure involved in this Ethical Zone.

MARKETING IMPLICATIONS

AN EXAMPLE OF the power that Authority and brands can have on convincing people to do things can be found in the experiments that Stanley Milgram did in the 1960s. As you may remember, the Milgram experiments convinced many of its participants to give very high (potentially lethal) electric shocks to another person. While we know in retrospect that the shocks were fake, and the "victim" was a confederate of the actor who was posing as a researcher, the research subjects didn't know. They were influenced by a white man in an experimenter's white coat—a typical Authority figure. The subjects afterward said that they went through with giving shocks even though they felt uneasy because they didn't want to let the experimenter down. They believed the experimenter wouldn't have them do something that was really bad, and they didn't want to ruin the experiment.

This observation gives an interesting insight into Authority. They trusted the authority figure to tell them the right thing to do. But there is also a brand lesson here: In one variation the experimenter varied the name of the school for which the experiment was being conducted, Yale or the University of Bridgeport. There was a difference in subjects being willing to give shocks by brand. As the stronger brand, Yale was more powerful in producing compliance.

Another researcher has followed up on Milgram's experiments and discovered that our brain waves are different when we are following orders than when we make a conscious choice. The Ethical Zone of Respect for Authority is very powerful and represents another way to emotionally brand your product.

Like a leader who is trustworthy, brands can be trusted to provide a consistent experience. So, in that sense, brands hold Authority. The desire for consistency that Conservatives hold is the key factor that explains why Conservatives prefer established brands, while Liberals favor the novelty of emerging new brands. Liberals crave novelty, Conservatives don't. By definition, Conservatives "conserve" the past. In contrast, Liberals are perennial early adopters, always looking for the next thing. This puts a different spin on the typical brand adoption cycle, where a new brand will get tried by the innovators and early adopters and then move to the mainstream and finally the late adopters. The Conservatives will be in the late majority and laggards, and by then the Liberal early adopters will have moved on to another product (as shown in the figure).

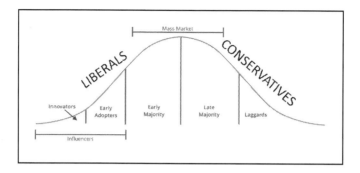

Those products that successfully make that shift from early majority to late majority must perform a balancing act because they inevitably will start to lose Liberals as they attempt to attract Conservatives. And Conservatives won't make the shift to a new product if the brand has been emotionally branded as Liberal.

Further, these Conservative later adopters aren't as curious as the Liberal earlier adopters and tend to not seek out information in general. Instead, they listen to the opinions of people in their in-group. They are open to social proof, but not in-depth information. Thus, in order to make the leap into the next stage of growth, brands need to shift from providing information for curious, novelty-seeking earlier adopters to providing social proof for stability-seeking Conservative later adopters all while not getting branded as just for Liberals.

UNDERSTAND THE POWER AND ENDURANCE OF EMOTIONAL BRANDING

TO ILLUSTRATE HOW this plays out in the brand landscape, let's look at two beverage brands, Pepsi and Coke. As we just discussed, as brands they both hold Authority, but these brands are emotionally branded in very different ways.

Pepsi's emotional branding efforts started with the campaign called "The Choice of a New Generation," which ran from 1984 to 1991, and has continued. Pepsi isn't *just* focusing on a demographic; it is focusing on a mind set that young people tend to have, Liberal and rebellious. Specifically, Pepsi is focusing on those who are low in Respect for Authority. Most recently, this was illustrated in the Kylie Jenner Pepsi commercial that incorporated an anti-authority pretend Black Lives

Matter march. That particular commercial didn't work well, for reasons I will discuss shortly.

Despite this correct match of mind set, age group, and an Ethical Zone, it seems that Pepsi hasn't been successful in attracting the young people of today. According to data from Connexity cited in an article in *Adweek*, Pepsi's largest audience is those over sixty-five. How can that be? It is probably because they are attracting Liberals, regardless of age. Why aren't they attracting young people? Both Liberals (and young people) crave novelty and are drinking the latest hip drinks like kombucha and not the boring colas that have been around since *forever*. Pepsi has recognized this and is attempting to capitalize on it by acquiring newer brands such as SoBe and Naked Juice. But Pepsi's customer base for its flagship brand seems to be limited to the aging Liberals who still retain a taste for colas.

By pursuing this emotional branding, Pepsi is experiencing the effects of the inherent tension of targeting Liberals: Pepsi is more attractive to those with Liberal sensibility than Coke, but as a brand with Authority and consistency, it is *never* going to satisfy the Liberal need for novelty. While the data firm Connexity recommended that Pepsi pursue young people, as an established brand with Authority and with a consistent product, that is probably not possible. Pepsi has successfully emotionally branded, but the branding has an inherent limit to growth.

The tension between a brand with Authority and the relatively low level of Respect for Authority among its Liberal user base is also illustrated in the reaction to the Pepsi Kylie Jenner campaign. Instead of feeling that Pepsi identified with its sensibilities, Liberals felt that Pepsi had co-opted the movement, attempting to use it to sell a product. As I discuss more fully later in the Care/Harm chapter, Liberals have a bullshit detector for companies "taking advantage" of an underprivileged group, which reflects both their Care/Harm and Fairness Ethical Zones (explained more in later chapters).

This is a "crime" among Liberals. A similar issue came up as part of the reaction to Nike's Colin Kaepernick campaign, that this was just being done to make money. Kaepernick defused the issue by donating his proceeds to charity; Nike hasn't. Being co-opted is a theme; it also comes up when big brand companies buy hip smaller brands. Pepsi is on a difficult path. Pepsi thought they were being on trend, but they ran into a marketing landmine they didn't know existed—and the explosion back-fired on them.

Let's move to Coke. According to that same data source, the Coke brand has the reverse skew. Its customer base is younger (the largest demographic group is thirty-five to forty-four) but skews right politi-cally. Coke's user base over-indexes Conservative by anywhere from ten to twenty-one percent. It also has a higher level of education than Pepsi. This is a mirror of Pepsi, another mismatch between age, education, and political skew. The correlations usually go the other way; in general, those more highly educated and younger skew Liberal. Coke's pattern is the reverse. Huh? What's going on here?

It could just be that it is a reverse of Pepsi, which still carries the long-term effect of the "Choice of a New Generation" campaign. Or it could be that Coke is the dominant brand and has done a better job of block-ing and tackling than Pepsi. Their 2014 campaign with 250 of the most popular names on Coke cans and bottles was a brilliant tactic, consid-ered to be one of the best-performing campaigns they have ever done. But their success among Conservatives also might be a long-term effect of the New Coke fiasco. For those who don't remember, in 1986, Coke changed its formula to a sweeter profile, trying to take on Pepsi in a dif-ferent way. It backfired, bigly. Conservatives (reminder, they want con-sistency) were probably more troubled by the change than Liberals.

After the publicity storm, Coke overturned their decision and brought back "Original Coke." By going back to the original formula, Coke probably cemented its lead among Conservatives. A long-term echo of this effect may still be playing out. And with Pepsi chasing Lib-erals, a Conservative cola drinker wouldn't choose Pepsi because of the Belonging Ethical Zone. Thus, both products are emotionally branded according to politics. I doubt Coca-Cola expected their Original Coke decision to end up emotionally branding the drink for Conservatives, but that appears to have been what happened.

AUTHORITY HELPS PEOPLE MAKE SENSE OF THE WORLD

ANOTHER PART OF what Respect for Authority does is this: You don't have to work to make sense of the world and what is good; it is done for you. It is easier to give over agency for your own life to an authority figure. It is uncomfortable to have to make your own decisions, to take responsibility for your own decisions when you might be wrong. If that were the case, you would be to blame for what is wrong with your life. It feels more difficult to make your own choices. Doing what you are told to do may lead to greater happiness (religious people are on average happier than those who are not) and lead to less anxiety (Liberals are more anxious than Conservatives).

A sentence in a 2017 job posting for a pastor wanted for a church in West Virginia illustrates some of this thinking: "We want a pastor who will tell us what to think and believe." That's a revealing statement about the Respect for Authority Ethical Zone. This Conservative congregation also had included that they wanted a leader who believed in the inerrancy of the Bible, so they weren't open to new beliefs (no novelty for us Conservatives!).

The ad for the pastor is certainly different from what one would read for a religious congregation in my home state of New Jersey, which has more Liberals. When we marketers create advertising by doing research with people who live and work in major cities, we probably aren't truly reflecting the values of Conservative America. We aren't aware that by doing so we aren't addressing a major part of the US, the part that made Donald Trump president.

It's difficult to make sense of the world—the world is a chaotic place with no consistency. I realize that statement takes a Liberal point of view. A Conservative would have written that God makes sense of this world, He is the force behind everything. I don't want to preach at you about theology; I just want to say that as a brand planner or marketer or creative or insight professional, you need to be aware of that difference, which should be integrated in the way you talk to your target audience. Most books on this topic are written by atheists, but they don't have the same insight that those of us who are not atheists have.

The high need for cognitive closure means that Conservatives are not open to ambiguity or nuance. They aren't going to sit still for a complicated explanation. They will go with the tried-and-true that they trust (remember they have motivated reasoning). This is their Achilles heel that makes them susceptible to fake news. It also tells you as a brand planner that Liberals need more information than Conservatives. The needs of your target audience should determine the length of your content.

IMPLICATIONS OF LEADERSHIP RESEARCH FOR BRANDING

LEADERSHIP EXPERTS SASHKIN and Sashkin have identified five key elements of leadership: attention, communication, trust, respect, and risk. Attention and communication obviously apply to marketing, but these theories don't add anything to the usual brand marketing rules. In marketing, trusting a brand is also relevant. The keys to developing trust as a leader are consistency and dependability (also important to a brand), but we know from the Ethical Frames model that consistency and dependability are even more important to customers who are Conservative than to Liberals.

The concept of respect is grounded in respecting relationships, which seems relevant to a brand. It can be difficult to be respectful when your worldview is different. Lack of respect can be diagnosed as condescension and disdain.

Finally, the element of risk refers to actions to get people involved in new activities. Because change is uncomfortable for Conservatives, if your brand is going to make a change, it is more important to engage them in any change effort because of that, and it is also important to emphasize the ways in which things are not changing. Your brand has to help Conservatives with change.

THE REBELS

THE FLIP SIDE of Respect for Authority is rebellion and anarchy. Words like *opposition*, *protest*, *refuse*, and *obstruct* capture more of the flavor of this. But it can be a little subtler. In conversations with Liberals, I heard the same comment repeatedly: "I respect authority when it is earned/justified/deserved."

Judging whether a leader is worthy of being followed may be a relatively recent change. In his 1977 book *Servant Leadership*, Robert Greenleaf claimed that Respect for Authority has been declining over time, noting that the campus protests and disrespect for Authority arose out of antiwar protests. Those who grew up in the sixties were rebelling against Authority and associated power with exploitation and evil.

The Volkswagen Beetle and its iconic "Think Small" ad provide a great example of a brand that appealed to those who were rebelling (read: younger and low in Respect for Authority) and repelled those who were high in Authority (read: Conservatives and older people) who would be attracted to big and powerful cars. Both the ad and the car say, "I am rejecting your values of respecting Authority". The sixties were only the start of this rebellion. The phrase "Speak Truth to Power" represents the current manifestation of this belief.

When searching online for ads in this theme, I found an ad for LGBTQ travel that took an iconic monument (Mount Rushmore) and showed their backsides—clearly a rebellious ad that is low in Respect for Authority.

But even those who rebel have leaders. The Black Panther movement had Bobby Seale and Huey Newton. The antivaccine movement has leaders such as Gwyneth Paltrow and Jenny McCarthy. Black Lives Matter had leaders. Due to the greater desire for novelty among the left, there is probably less attachment to individual leaders than among the right and they have less ability to get people to do things, but they still do have leaders who are influential. The Occupy Wall Street movement was perhaps less successful in coalescing into a long-term movement because they attempted to work without leaders out of extremely low Respect for Authority. Authority has value; anarchy makes it more difficult to accomplish things.

A leader isn't a leader unless he or she has followers, and there needs to be a match between the followers and the leader. But leaders work only because of followers; they are mutually dependent.

But how does a leader lead when people are low in Respect for Authority? It's tricky. As we just saw, those who study leadership have concluded effective leaders today have to not just deal with the traditional items of tasks and relationship, they also have to deal with change.

Transparency is often viewed as the antidote to leaders who can't be trusted by those who are low in Respect for Authority. It doesn't increase respect but is viewed as a check on unbridled power. Thus, theoretically, transparency would be more important to Liberals than to Conservatives. This is a hypothesis, and I would love to see a test of this.

PATRIARCHY AS AUTHORITY

As I HAVE been writing this book, I have been acutely aware of pronouns. In the developed world, leaders are men. This is described by academia and the left as "patriarchy." Power in Western society is now and has in the past been held by men, usually white men. Thus, ads that feature an older white male (such as Dr. Marcus Welby, who also had the doctor status, which enhances his Authority) emotionally brand for those who are high in Respect for Authority, such as Conservatives.

In contrast, the left views the power being held by men as illegitimate, purely an artifact of the past, reinforcing and justifying their low Respect for Authority perceptions. The #MeToo movement has pointed out the way that some men exploited their power and Authority, as has the ongoing Catholic priest sex abuse scandals. These are abuses of power, betraying the responsibility a leader has to his followers.

It remains to be seen if these recent events will result in a shift in attitudes beyond the progressive left just as the sixties rebellion did. On the Liberal side, note that many of the authority figures of the antivaccine movement are women. Ads that use women in general, and also black men, are going to be more attractive to Liberal viewers than to Conservatives. Unfortunately, race also matters, which will be discussed in more detail in the Sacredness chapter.

MONEY AND POWER AND AUTHORITY

MONEY AND WEALTH are key signifiers of Authority. People with money have more power. Having a higher salary as a CEO, dictator, or preacher can act to bolster Authority and is one reason why people seek money (beyond craving what it can buy). Conservatives are less likely to be against people earning lots of money and may actually view with pride how well-off those in Authority are because they believe it reflects well on them that their leader is successful. On the other hand, those on the left are more likely to be upset about high pay because, to them, the Ethical Zone of Fairness is higher in importance than Respect for Authority. (I'll discuss this more in the chapter on Fairness.)

Speaking of money, it's not surprising that those with high need for cognitive closure (read: Conservatives) are less likely to make changes to their investments such as rebalancing, as is recommended. They stick with what they believe! Only those who have hired a financial advisor (an Authority), have rebalanced their portfolios, which has been shown to lead to better financial results. Thus, high Respect for Authority helps Conservatives to overcome some of the limitations of their HNFCC thinking style.

MORE MARKETING IMPLICATIONS

BY EXAMINING THE principles of leadership developed by experts in light of the Authority Ethical Zone, we can conclude that brands must deliver the product benefits (task), have a relationship with their customer or consumer (relationship), and deal with change. How to deal with change is tricky because it means different things for different customers. For a Conservative customer, dealing with change mostly means staving off change by consistency, which generally mean consistent quality and price. For a Liberal customer, dealing with change might mean dealing with their desire for novelty. Thus, Starbucks (which appeals more to fickle Liberal customers) needs to change their blends and flavors more often than Dunkin' Donuts, which appeals more to Conservatives who don't want things to change. Trader Joe's constantly changing its product mix is a match for its Liberal customer base, but such practices would be a disaster at Kroger.

Lower levels of Respect for Authority can be used to emotionally brand with the concepts of empowerment and agency. This is the Ethical Zone employed in the Always Maxi Pads "Empower" ad campaign, which talks about empowering girls to go beyond the limitations that society has placed on them. Other brands that have similar emotional branding are Keds ("It's a run the world shoe"—with a picture of women), Neutrogena ("It's our job at Neutrogena to put her best face forward" with a picture of a black woman), and Olay ("~~Too~~ outspoken. When I speak, I will be heard" on a billboard in Times Square with a picture of a black woman).

As I mentioned earlier, by emotionally branding using low Respect for Authority, these brands might be setting off a marketing landmine among Conservatives. They are confronting the opposite belief among the half of Conservatives that women should remain in their place; a Conservative viewer would probably believe that the limitations on girls' activities that Always promises to go beyond are valid and should be respected.

Brand marketers need to recognize that they are putting their own lower Respect for Authority values into their campaigns and that may not always match the values of their target audience or of watchers. Given the fact that Always marketer P&G is located in the more Conservative Midwest, it is somewhat surprising that they made that decision, but it probably reflects big-city Cincinnati values and not rural Ohio. The Always campaign to empower girls directly strikes at the forces behind patriarchy, so I think Conservatives would feel that it challenges the order they support. This campaign has run for three decades and is considered successful, but I suspect Always brand sales are weaker among Conservatives. Even though Conservatives tend to be men and older, there are Conservative young women, and I can't imagine them believing that being empowered by a sanitary napkin is valuable.

Coors ran into a marketing landmine when they tried to emotionally brand using low Respect for Authority with their "Climb on" campaign, which portrayed people, including women (!), overcoming challenges. They were trying to bond with a new target audience of under-thirty-fives, and, at first, the campaign was touted as a success, with awareness and brand sales up among the new target. But the following year, they killed the campaign after *overall* brand sales fell by four-percent. Did the low Respect for Authority (as illustrated by women achieving things beyond what they are "supposed to") turn off their core Conservative drinker? The campaign was replaced by one that highlights a Conservative emotional branding theme: the Coors Rocky Mountain heritage—a strategy that is powered by the Ethical Zones of Belonging (the national heritage message) and Authority (consistency).

I am not telling you what decision your brand should make, merely to be aware of where the marketing landmines are and to figure out how to use them for emotional branding.

Direct-to-consumer advertising for pharmaceutical drugs is another type of ad that encourages empowerment. Data from Connexity validates this: Customers who shop at CVS stores and who skew Conservative say they are less willing to challenge their doctor on a prescription than the Liberals who shop at CVS online. My own research shows that Conservatives feel educating doctors is more important than Liberals do, probably because doctors are Authority figures who need to be well-informed.

On the other hand, Liberals are more curious and more likely to seek out their own information, which is why they don't feel it is as important as Conservatives do that doctors be educated about drugs. AbbVie's campaign for its new endometriosis product, where they try to empower women to challenge their doctor in order to get out of a cycle of misdiagnosis, will probably be more successful among Liberal women than among Conservatives.

REVISITING EARLIER EXAMPLES

I PROMISED TO come back to the three brands, Nike, Dick's, and Bonobos, to look at how Respect for Authority contributed to the marketing landmines:

- In taking a knee during the national anthem, Colin Kaepernick (and the others, and Nike by extension) was defying the owners, mostly white men, who represent Authority. Then, President Trump weighed in, suggesting that the NFL create a policy that would basically fire any player who took a knee. With the president making comments, there is another Authority figure commenting, giving the issue increased importance for Conservatives. That's double violation of the Ethical Zone of Respect for Authority. This operates in two different ways: as an emotional branding device for those low in Respect for Authority and as a landmine for those high in Respect for Authority.
- The reaction to Dick's Sporting Goods not selling assault rifles could have been quieted by an authority figure, which could

have happened if President Trump had come out in support of Dick's or of gun-control, but he didn't. President Trump has wavered on gun issues, so the marketing landmine that Dick's wandered into doesn't have that Ethical Zone behind it.

- On the other hand, the Bonobos #EvolvetheDefinition definitely violated the Ethical Zone of Respect for Authority. The campaign challenges the underpinnings of patriarchy just by the range of who is included in the commercial (nonwhite, nonstraight men). The Belonging and Community and Respect for Authority Ethical Zones reinforce each other to inflame passions against this commercial even more. Again, this works as an emotional branding device for low in Respect for Authority, and as a landmine for those who are high in Respect for Authority.

There's more analysis of these brands coming in the next chapter so you can more fully understand how each of the various Ethical Zones contribute to emotional marketing landmines.

CULTURAL DIFFERENCES

TO GIVE YOU a flavor of some of the differences culturally, Germans and Japanese are both higher in Respect for Authority than people in the US and the UK. African countries are also higher, which may explain their tendency to allow strongmen to come to power. The 2018 election of the autocratic new Brazilian president, Jair Bolsonaro, is another example of this Ethical Zone at work. Any campaign that is intended to be used globally needs to consider the variations in the importance of the various Ethical Zones and how they are interpreted in various cultures.

CONSOLIDATING WHAT WE LEARNED

JUST LIKE BELONGING and Community, Respect for Authority is an evolutionarily important zone of human experience. A high level of Respect for Authority tends to be associated with desire for order and conscientiousness, two of the five key variables of personality, a high need for cognitive closure, and a gloomy worldview, which plays out in how people parent. Those with high levels of Respect for Authority also are resistant to change (a key element of being Conservative); those who have lower levels have a high desire for novelty. The rebelliousness of the 1960s has loosened Respect for Authority, although some people (especially Conservatives in the US) still have high levels. Patriarchy is a key part of Respect for Authority and empowering those who are disadvantaged may be perceived as challenging the power of patriarchy/Authority, which can backfire if your target audience is Conservative.

A key element of brands is that they do hold Authority. Chain restaurants and existing packaged goods brands are stronger among Conservatives. Authority can be used in emotional branding either with those who are low or those who are high, but can set up marketing landmines if we aren't aware of this Ethical Zone. Applying research on leadership to the concept of Authority and brands tells us that brands need to help them manage change: For Liberals, brands need to provide the novelty they seek; for Conservatives, brands need to provide consistency or prepare them for change. Those in Authority need to be matched with the type of followers they have, and they have to have both respect and responsibility for their followers. Transparency is viewed as an antidote to untrustworthy leaders among those who are low in Respect for Authority but it does not lead to trust.

CHAPTER 3

WHAT IS IMPORTANT: SACREDNESS, PURITY, AND DISGUST

W HAT DO ALL these ads have in common?

- A Mike's Hard Lemonade ad showing an industrial accident, with a large metal object protruding from a man's body
- A Coors Light commercial showing "hot chicks running around at parties"
- A feminine hygiene ad
- A toilet paper commercial with a bear using the product
- A man opening a beer bottle with his butt

The answer is that the five ads were all rated as disgusting by college students, who are typically Liberals.

The third of the five Ethical Zones is that of Sacredness. I've added the label to the third bubble in the Ethical Frames model.

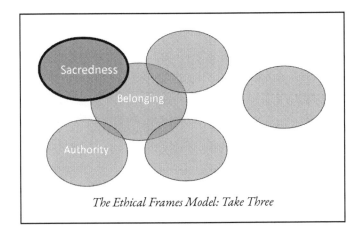

The Ethical Frames Model: Take Three

Just like Belonging and Authority, Sacredness developed from our evolutionary history. Having food that is safe to eat (not poisonous, not contaminated) was key to survival. Societies that survived developed ways to identify those foods that were safe and unsafe; we are all descended from them. (Do you see a theme? So far, all three of the Ethical Zones we have talked about have been part of our evolutionary history. We need to appreciate what they did for us.)

DISGUST AS AN INDICATOR OF VIOLATION

THE PHYSIOLOGICAL MECHANISM that developed to distinguish which foods were safe was disgust. Disgust is one of the basic emotions found in all cultures. It evokes the physical response of nausea. The signature disgust look was described centuries ago by Charles Darwin as having three elements: a gaping mouth with an upper lip retraction and a nose wrinkle. More recent experts have proposed some variations. Neurological research demonstrates that the region of the brain that is activated by disgust is the anterior insula.

Having a physical aversion to things that might kill you also helps you to survive. Part of this survival mechanism is cleanliness. "Cleanliness is next to Godliness" captures one element of the Sacredness zone. Thus, cleaning products belong in this zone. Personally, I am relatively low in this Ethical Zone, so it took me a while to figure out that the word *filth* to describe things that were messy, but not literally dirty, is a tip-off that the other person was high in Sacredness.

In addition to having safe food, most societies developed some concept of the Sacred, of God, or of a Higher Power. To explain why societies have this idea in common, theorists suggest that we humans automatically perceive a "hierarchy of social space," with the higher levels representing moral purity, or God, then animals, and, finally, the lowest levels of depravity or the devil. Evolutionarily, having a shared concept of the Divine bound together societies and this may have also helped them survive.

What ties together these ideas are the feelings we get when Sacredness norms are violated, disgust. "That's disgusting" is a clear tip-off that you are operating in the Sacredness Ethical Zone, even if you aren't talking about food. In fact, the mouth being involved in a disgust expression even in non-food-related situations is regarded as evidence that the emotion of disgust originated out of the need to avoid contaminated foods and poisons. Another theorist suggests that disgust may also signal that Community defining norms are being violated. Ideas that help promote group cohesion were to be prized, and ideas that threaten the group were to be abhorred. Regardless of why or how it occurs, academic research has confirmed that inhibiting nausea with drugs reduces the *moral* disgust reaction.

One hallmark of disgust is the idea it might spread, using words such as *contamination*, *viral*, or *epidemic*. There's an element of dangerousness about lack of Sacredness, a lack of safety.

EXAMPLES OF THE SACREDNESS ETHICAL ZONE

WHAT MAKES THE Ethical Zone of Sacredness confusing is that different societies and cultures place different interpretations on this zone. In the US, Conservatives and Liberals react very differently based on what they believe is Sacred.

You can see by the examples of Liberal Sacredness cited at the beginning of the chapter that the college kids held as Sacred treating all people well and perhaps treat as Sacred the disadvantaged (this will be discussed further in the next chapter). Opposition to the death penalty because life is Sacred is a way of talking about this Ethical Zone among Liberals. Calling a certain way of eating "clean" taps into this zone among Liberals.

"Eat Clean Bro" is an "all natural prepared meal" kit service. The phrase "Clean Plate" is used as a restaurant name, as a brand name for a cleaning product, and a website with the promotional line: "Find healthy food, delicious recipes, nutrition news, and wellness tips at Clean Plates, plus great new food products and restaurants for clean eating." Organic food is viewed as pure. A vegetarian sausage company that has branded itself "No evil" is also drawing on this Ethical Zone.

Liberals view foods made with GMOs as disgusting. I once heard someone say GMO food isn't real food. Yellow rice, which has been genetically modified to provide beta-carotene for malnourished people in developing countries, has not been distributed because of the GMO Sacredness Ethical Zone issue. Besides food, this Ethical Zone influences health decisions. Research has demonstrated that antivaccine attitudes are stronger among mothers who are high in Sacredness, even among Liberals.

On the other side, Conservatives hold as Sacred religion, marriage, families, chastity, scripture, and certain music. The phrase "body is a temple" illustrates the right's emphasis. An ad for an abortion clinic would qualify as disgusting for Conservatives. An ad campaign for a Merck vaccine for HPV (which said that parents have an obligation to protect their children against cancer caused by sexually transmitted diseases) has been called disgusting, presumably among the right because of its implication of lack of sex purity. I haven't found a list of ads that the right finds disgusting, but one published academic study mentioned that even "impure" thoughts can cause disgust among those who are religious. While there is a lot of individual variability among people, Conservatives in general have higher sensitivity to disgust.

MARKETING IMPLICATIONS

MANY PRODUCT CATEGORIES are already in the Sacredness zone, either in the positive or the negative. The domains of disgust described by Rozin and Haidt are one way to tell whether your product is in the Sacredness Zone:

- Food products
- Body related products

- Animals
- Sexual behaviors (including homosexuality)
- Death, illness or corpses
- Exterior body breaches (such as rashes, gashes, blemishes and deformity)
- Poor hygiene and sanitation
- Social order violations which can elicit moral disgust (example: cheating)

Thus, advertisers in food, scents, cleaning products and bodily waste categories are operating in this Ethical Zone. Drugs for disfiguring diseases are also, as are the opposite, beauty products. While advertisers in these categories have learned to navigate this Ethical Zone, they can still make mistakes, such as the toilet paper bear commercial on the college students' list.

Obviously, this has implications for food and restaurant businesses. Food illness outbreaks, such as the ones experienced at Chipotle, awaken our disgust reflex. Although some may think that showing the actual ingredients may be a way of reassuring people as to their Sacredness and purity, one academic study demonstrated that showing raw meat awakens the disgust reflex. That doesn't seem to be the answer. To address the Sacredness Ethical Zone, some food companies have developed codes that provide information on where the food was sourced.

The trend toward crystals reflects the use of the Sacredness Ethical Zone in product development. Urban Outfitters sells four different types of crystal clusters. Besides the use of crystals as healing modalities and as Sacred objects, they are being incorporated into marketing and actual products for women: Sephora and Estée Lauder are using gemstone terminology, and Sephora is offering a pearl mask and rose quartz luminizer.

A FLOP FOLLOWED BY A WIN

DISFIGURING DISEASES ARE automatically in the Sacredness Ethical Zone. One product provides a great case study of how it used this Zone in two different ways, with different results: the prescription drug Lamisil from Novartis for toenail fungus. First, Novartis developed a consumer ad to promote that toenails would look pretty if you used Lamisil, a use of the positive side of the Sacredness Ethical Zone. (Full disclosure: Although I was working at Novartis during part of this time, I did not work on this product. This account comes from published sources.)

This was a flop. It wasn't motivating enough to overcome the barriers that doctors had of prescribing a systemic medication with side effects to treat a local problem. Next, they developed a new campaign with a cartoon depiction of the fungus, a disgusting-looking creature. It was so disgusting that a search today over a decade later still finds it mentioned on lists of the most disgusting ad campaigns ever. This second campaign was much more successful, increasing sales whenever they ran the ad. For Lamisil, the disgusting negative was much more motivating than the positive of Sacredness (as represented by beauty).

The emotional power of disgust has been confirmed in an academic study that found disgust was more motivating than fear. Violating the Sacredness Ethical Zone in advertising can be an effective way to emotionally brand.

OTHER WAYS SACREDNESS IS USED IN ADVERTISING

THERE ARE SIGNATURE colors for Sacredness. A search for "pure" images on Google resulted in pictures of white roses, clear blue water, and women in white bridal dresses. There's a reason why Mr. Clean's clothes stay white as he cleans. White is the color of Sacredness and purity—think bridal dresses, Ivory soap that is "99% pure," and Neutrogena soap that is so clear you can see through it. Nivea used the color associated with this Ethical Zone to emotionally brand when it used the line "white is purity."

Similarly, when I did a test of colors for an asthma inhaler, white was the color with the highest ratings for safety—connoting a lack of dangerousness. Blue was next (both colors that relate to this zone). Transparency can also indicate purity; Johnson & Johnson's decision to take the yellow color out of its baby shampoo is a move to emotionally brand using this Ethical Zone, as are clear plastic egg cartons.

I once did market research on a powerful ad that illustrated intense pain by superimposing a pattern of shattered glass over a knee. That image made people so uncomfortable that the brand manager toned it down by changing the color of the shattered-glass pattern from red to blue. The implied violation of the skin tapped into the Sacredness Ethical Zone, and the blue color softened the impact because it counteracted the implied violation.

An ad can inadvertently touch the Sacredness Ethical Zone in other ways, such as using women in an objectifying way, which provokes outrage from Liberals as an interpersonal offense. A Pinterest page devoted to disgusting ads includes ads with human and animal waste, and ads that use women in sexist and demeaning ways.

In the previously mentioned study that asked college students to identify two ads that they found disgusting, the major categories were these: "gross" depictions (such as the metal object protruding from a man's body) as well as ads that were "indecent, sexually oriented, sexist and sexually objectifying portrayals," such as the Coors beer hot chicks ad mentioned in the opening of this chapter. A recent IKEA ad that offered a discount on cribs for pregnant women if they urinated on the print ad (to reveal the discount) may have also provoked a disgust response, especially among those who are high in purity.

Unfortunately, it seems that fat people also violate societal standards and the Sacredness Ethical Zone. The Pinterest page of disgusting ads had several pictures of fat people, with excess flesh bulging out in extreme ways. Dove's emotional branding device of using "real" women who don't meet the societal standards of being anorexically thin would probably appeal more to those who are low in the Sacredness zone.

Nonprofits use disgust in ads relatively often, perhaps more often than profit-making companies do. An academic study on the effectiveness of using disgust in advertising used images from the Montana Meth Project, an award-winning campaign that uses images such as a teenager with open sores on his face. When reviewing ad compendiums on the internet, I found a lot of nonprofit ads with revolting imagery. One of those was an ad from the World Wildlife Fund of a woman pulling a suitcase through the airport leaving a trail of blood, with the headline, "Don't buy exotic animal souvenirs."

PREJUDICE AND SACREDNESS

THERE'S AN ELEPHANT in this chapter that I need to address: the issue of the "other," racial and sexual prejudice issues. This is a touchy subject, so I will try my best not to offend anyone, but this is difficult, so please read with kind eyes. I am not saying that this is right; I am describing what the research says. Don't shoot the messenger.

The Sacredness zone is a contributing factor to racial and sexual prejudice. Other zones may be involved (especially the "othering" that was referenced in the chapter on Belonging and Community). The tip-off that tells you which Ethical Zone is involved can be found in the language being used. When the Nazis used the words *racial purity*, they were invoking the Sacredness zone. When immigrants are called "animals" who are "infesting" the rest of the country, the person is operating in the Sacredness zone. When women in some societies are considered unclean when they are menstruating (in some developing countries they must leave their house during menstruation), this is the Sacredness zone. The disgusted reaction to the feminine hygiene ad by the college students is the developed world equivalent to the menstruating women issue.

The US history of slavery was justified based on bogus reasoning that slaves were less than fully human (note that this means they are lower on the Sacredness scale). The previously mentioned Nivea ad with the tagline "white is purity" referring to its product was appropriated by some hate groups for use because of the prejudice associated with this Ethical Zone. Because Nivea was only thinking about its product, and not about the other aspects of this Ethical Zone, the company didn't realize that the ad could be interpreted differently.

Regardless of Nivea's original intent, because this Ethical Zone does encompass race, some people on the right took advantage of Nivea's ad. I say those on the right because Conservatives are more sensitive to race. But even white Europeans, who do not have the same history of slavery as we do in the U.S.A., show a greater likelihood to associate images of black people with words like *evil* and *bad* in the implicit bias test (a test of the level of prejudice someone has). And images of people of another race are more likely to be perceived as threatening than those of the same race. This reflects the Sacredness Ethical Zone.

These reactions have a deep origin and may, in fact, be innate. Psychologists have done studies with young children (as young as six months) to see where they spend more time gazing, and they spend more time looking at pictures of people that are like the ones they see every day, people of the same race. (Note: If children are raised by caregivers of a different race before age eight, their brains act as though they were of the race of the caregiver. If they join the different-race caregivers after age eight, they don't.) The researchers who did the study of infant gazing interpret it to mean that, as humans, we have innate preferences for those who are like us.

This finding may partially explain what is involved in the Sacredness Ethical Zone. Another study among adults showed that different areas of our brain are engaged when we see someone of the same race versus someone of a different race. But studies also find that as people become more educated and more exposed to others who are different in a positive way, those prejudices start to erode. Those who have college educations are lower in the Sacredness Ethical Zone than those who have less education. They are using both their rational brains and another Ethical Zone (discussed in the next chapter) to overcome what may be an innate human preference for people like ourselves. In fact, a recent study found that young, white Liberals actually have a slight preference for those who are of another race.

In general, because Conservatives are higher in both Sacredness and the Belonging Ethical Zones they are more likely to be higher in racial prejudice. There has been a trend to show mixed racial groupings in advertising, which may be received differently by people with different sensitivities to the Sacredness zone. Liberals will be more positive toward this, while Conservatives may not be. Thus, the race of your ad's cast is part of your emotional branding.

This doesn't mean that *all* Liberals and Conservatives are this way, because there is wide variability in the dispersion of the zones. For example, someone I know who is very high on the Sacredness zone calls himself "left of Michael Moore." Similarly, many antivaccine advocates who are high in the Ethical Zone of Sacredness are Liberals.

Again, these aren't my attitudes. I do not believe the prejudice associated with this Ethical Zone is good. I personally have been working to vanquish my own implicit bias. I am only describing what the research says. You may be tempted to continue to preach or rail against those who are prejudiced, but this Ethical Zone and its psychological and biological underpinnings are part of why preaching doesn't work. But don't get discouraged. Even though you can't change people's prejudice, you can change people's minds about specific issues. Be sure to check out the Reframing chapter for details.

Finally, it may be that this part of the Ethical Zone is flexible and can encompass other ideas. It may be that democracy or liberty is viewed as Sacred, or even owning guns. Lots of research could be done in this area It is important for you to know how this concept touches your product space.

REVISITING EARLIER EXAMPLES

YOU CAN PROBABLY see that the Sacredness Ethical Zone is involved in Nike's Colin Kaepernick issue, just because it is about black men—both those who are taking a knee during the national anthem and the black men who are being killed. A similar issue is involved in the Bonobos pants campaign, because gays and transpeople also hold a lower position in the Sacredness Ethical Zone hierarchy. So, all three of these Ethical Zones, which are higher among Conservatives, are activated by these two campaigns, magnifying the marketing landmines these brands encountered.

The Parkland shooting/Dick's Sporting Goods gun control issue is slightly different. So far, it has only been the Belonging and Community Ethical Zone. But I wonder if guns have taken on a mythical importance among Conservatives and whether guns themselves have moved into the Sacredness Ethical Zone. That would certainly help to explain why the emotions run so high among Conservatives about this issue. This is an issue worth researching.

The combination of more than one marketing landmine yields a more powerful explosion.

The Sacredness Ethical Zone is a powerful emotional branding device. Some advertisers are already in it because of their product and some have borrowed it for branding. They need to understand it to use it well. Understanding this Ethical Zone more fully can help an advertiser avoid triggering it inadvertently or blundering in unaware and failing, like Nivea did. And be prepared for the power of the fallout of the marketing landmine if you do decide to go ahead.

CULTURAL DIFFERENCES

THIS CHAPTER HAS focused on WEIRD North American culture and how it experiences Sacredness and disgust. While much of the literature that discusses this has been done in English-speaking countries, all societies experience this Ethical Zone but differently. In India, the Ethical Zone of Sacredness affects perceptions of those of different castes, and represents a virtue to be protected, even by murder.

In Japan, as in North America, corruption violates the social order and is regarded as "dirty"—another tip-off that the Ethical Zone is Sacredness. The antidote to corruption is believed to be transparency, which fits in with the Sacredness Ethical Zone. Cross-cultural advertising needs to take care to avoid transgressing the culturally based Sacredness norms of the society.

CONSOLIDATING WHAT WE HAVE LEARNED

THE THIRD ETHICAL Zone has evolutionary history of Sacredness, purity, and disgustingness. This zone touches off different reactions in our brains and even manifests in how long infants stare at pictures of others. This zone derives evolutionarily from being able to discern safe food, and the signature expression of disgust indicating violation of this zone is a curled upper lip. This reaction has been generalized to animals, waste products, violating the body's boundaries, and even more broadly to those who violate society's moral code.

By virtue of the nature of their product, some advertising automatically touches this Ethical Zone; others use it as borrowed interest. Like the first two zones, this zone is stronger among Conservatives, but there are manifestations among Liberals as seen in the antivaccine movement and in "clean" food. Disgust can be used to emotionally brand a product, as illustrated in a case study of the prescription antifungal drug Lamisil and confirmed in academic research.

But as I discuss again later in the chapter on the Rules of Engagement, you need to be careful when you use disgust. This Ethical Zone is also the source of prejudice, which is signaled by language of infestation or infecting or dirty. Advertising employing this Ethical Zone can be misused or misappropriated by those who are prejudiced, another type of emotional marketing landmine. Other cultures have the same Zone; the interpretation varies, but the underlying concept is the same. Violating more than one Ethical Zone makes the marketing landmine even more powerful, as illustrated by the analysis of the underlying factors behind the reactions to the Nike, Dick's, and Bonobos issues.

CHAPTER 4

WHO GETS REWARDED? FAIRNESS AND MERIT

"It's not fair!"

Kids have a finely developed sense of Fairness, but it may not be what parents want to hear. A search of titles at my local library turns up several books for parents to use to teach their children about Fairness, but almost none for adults. The theme of the books is how children should share.

Books on Fairness aren't needed. Psychological research among young children (as young as three years old) demonstrates that children develop a sense of what is Fair very early. For kids, research has shown that what is Fair has two parts to it: equal shares when effort isn't involved (equality), and proportionate shares when effort is involved (merit). This is the fourth Ethical Zone: Fairness.

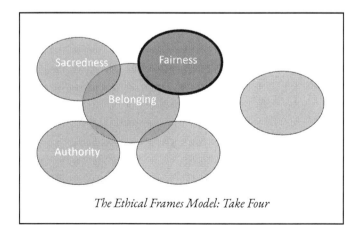

The Ethical Frames Model: Take Four

As an adult, when we think about the Fairness Ethical Zone, we each prefer one flavor. Conservatives place more emphasis on merit, while Liberals place more emphasis on equality. We usually only think about the one we prefer, not the other flavor of Fairness that kids have instinctively.

Because adults don't recognize as valid the other flavor of Fairness and because we use the same word to mean different things, the Ethical Zone of Fairness has become a source of major conflict in the United States. When someone says they are concerned about income inequality, the chances are high that they are a Liberal, because that is about equality. In fact, because the most Liberal among us recognize historical inequality and because they are extremely high on the Ethical Zone of Care/Harm, they sometimes favor giving more shares to those who are disadvantaged to make up for previous inequities. The interaction of these factors leads to a third flavor of Fairness: need. These different interpretations play out in our disagreements about health care, college admissions, job opportunities, and arrests and jail sentencing. The emphasis on the need-based flavor of Fairness is probably behind a recent change in preference among Liberals for those of other races.

The Fairness Ethical Zone interacts with the Belonging Ethical Zone. Those who have more of a merit flavor to their Fairness Ethical Zone will also believe that those in their in-group also deserve more. This is an element that binds groups together (and it is a good thing for groups to be bound together. Really! That's the positive side of Belonging.).

MARKETING IMPLICATIONS

THESE CONCEPTS ARE used in branding occasionally. It's not a major theme, but ads that use "deserve" or "worth it" are invoking the Fairness zone. One observer believes that two campaigns were behind the trend to use Fairness: the McDonald's "You Deserve a Break Today" campaign and the L'Oréal "You Are Worth It" campaign. This has led to other advertisers picking up on this theme and, some say, contributing to a shift to an entitlement culture.

This Ethical Zone is invoked ever so lightly when retailers provide benefits to their frequent customers, or to those who have loyalty cards. When a store requires that customers buy a certain combination of purchases or requires them to sign in before they get a discount, they are saying (implicitly) you have to work to get a special deal. That's the merit-flavor of Fairness.

Pricing is also another area where Fairness is involved. An ad for WaWa Convenience Stores, which promotes that all sizes of coffee are the same price, is using the equality-flavor of Fairness. When Walmart charges "everyday low prices," they are in the equality-flavored Fairness Ethical Zone. Other stores that vary the prices whether you are part of their loyalty program or have purchased a certain number of items (both relating to earning the discount, either by participation in a group or achieving something) are using the merit-flavor Ethical Zone.

Some drug manufacturers price their drugs so that all dosage strengths are priced the same, while others make it proportionate to the amount of drug in the pill, reflecting the two major flavors of Fairness. Theoretically, I would expect Liberals to be more in favor of Walmart's pricing system, and Conservatives to back the store loyalty program discounts, but I don't see any rhetoric to that effect. Instead, other Ethical Zones override the Fairness-related pricing perceptions. Perhaps putting more emphasis on the equality-flavor of Walmart's pricing could begin to make Liberals feel more positively toward the retailer.

Pricing spikes violate our sense of Fairness because they aren't based on either equality or merit. A store that raises the price of plywood after a hurricane, or a gas station that hikes the price of gas during a shortage are the targets of rage. Pharma exec (and now convicted felon) Martin Shkreli's price increase for Daraprim (a drug to treat a rare disease) generated ire both because it was such a large price increase (violating Conservatives' desire for consistency and order) and also because it was undeserved (violating Liberals' sense of Fairness). Shkreli didn't do anything except buy the drug.

Branded pharmaceutical companies who have spent years of effort and millions of dollars to develop new drugs still get pushback for their high prices, but nowhere near the outrage directed at Shkreli, perhaps because the *effort* behind the branded drugs at least somewhat justifies the high price (the merit-flavor of Fairness).

There are cultural variations of the Fairness zones, but I need to do more work to be able to summarize them. Stay tuned to my blog at www.ethicalframes.com, as I will post when I find research on this topic.

CONSOLIDATING WHAT WE HAVE LEARNED

THE FAIRNESS ETHICAL Zone has two main flavors: equality and merit. These appear to be instinctual, as demonstrated by research among very young children. Although we all have them both, as we come of age, we come to place more of an emphasis on one or the other. Conservatives favor the merit-flavor, while Liberals favor the equality-flavor. Another flavor of Fairness is becoming more popular among those on the political far left: that of making it up to those who haven't been treated equally or have need.

Conflicts arise when we don't recognize that the flavor of the Fairness Ethical Zone being used is different than our own. This Ethical Zone has been used occasionally in marketing but is used more often in making pricing decisions and when we require people to take an action to qualify for a benefit or discount, such as quantity or loyalty discounts. This Ethical Zone is also behind the outrage consumers feel for large price increases.

CHAPTER 5
WHEN HEARTS EXPLODE: CARE/HARM

"IF IT BLEEDS, it leads."

This phrase isn't just about violence; it refers to stories that tug on your heartstrings. Newspaper articles and television news in Liberal media regularly activate our Ethical Zone of Care/Harm, because they know that those articles and segments get more attention and evoke more emotion. This Ethical Zone is why statistics aren't as compelling as faces of those affected; statistics don't arouse our Care/Harm Ethical Zone. Activating the Care/Harm Ethical Zone causes our hearts to explode, can be used to emotionally brand, and creates an emotional marketing landmine.

This is the fifth Ethical Zone, Care/Harm, which I have added to the Ethical Frames model.

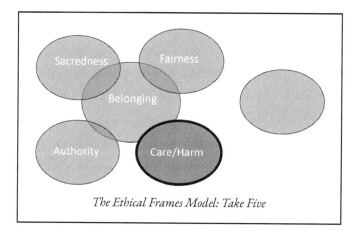

The Ethical Frames Model: Take Five

The importance placed on the Care/Harm Ethical Zone has grown as societies have become wealthier and more developed. Liberals place much more importance on the Care/Harm Ethical Zone. Children who are raised in Conservative families that are comfortable may develop greater emphasis on Care/Harm than their parents because of the sunnier worldview people develop when the world is more stable. This is part of a long-term trend of movement toward people becoming more Liberal, but since the Great Recession that began in 2008, this may have reversed.

EMPATHY: THE BASIS OF THE CARE/HARM ETHICAL ZONE

THE CARE/HARM ETHICAL Zone is based on humans' inborn tendency for empathy. One of the ways to study empathy and the lack of it is to look at those who lack it: psychopaths. Brain scans of criminal psychopaths show that they lack normal activity in regions of the brain that are now recognized to be the seat of empathy (the amygdala). Psychologists who study psychopaths use language about conscience, illustrating how we equate conscience with the Care/Harm Ethical Zone.

But just telling people they should have a conscience doesn't work; the amygdala is a part of the older reptile brain. This may be another reason why teaching ethics doesn't really change anything. A workshop on teaching ethics I attended tried to activate people's Care/Harm Ethical Zone using journaling, music videos, and scenes from movies. That wouldn't work if the person's amygdala wasn't responsive.

Literature about psychopaths focuses on the less than one-percent of the population who have committed egregious crimes and are in prison. Sometimes business people are labeled as psychopaths because they make decisions without considering the harm that they do to others. One study among businesspeople estimated that four-percent of them might be psychopaths. It's obviously not an actual diagnosis but instead reflects the harm that they perceive that businesses can do to people due to their lack of empathy. (This topic will be discussed further in a later chapter.)

Interestingly, two hormones affect the Care/Harm Ethical Zone. High levels of testosterone appear to block high levels of empathy, and high levels of oxytocin (the hormone that is released among mothers when they see pictures of their babies) promote high Care/Harm importance. Not surprisingly given the effect of hormones, women in general have higher levels of the Care/Harm Ethical Zone and are more likely to be Liberal. Again, just like the fact that Care/Harm is situated in the amygdala, this isn't something that can be changed.

The groups of people who have the strongest emphasis on Care/Harm are Liberals, and importance is strongest among the youngest. This powerful emotion can explode, especially among millennials who place particular importance on Care/Harm. It's not that Conservatives don't care about others; they place equal importance on all the Ethical Zones so they are less extreme than Liberals. Among Conservatives, the Care/Harm Ethical Zone interacts with the other Ethical Zones that are equally important to them (Belonging, Authority, and Sacredness), while for Liberals, Care/Harm mostly interacts with Fairness. Thus, it looks very different, even though both may be operating from the Care/Harm Ethical Zone. This is why Conservatives respond differently to the stories that "bleeding-heart" Liberals find compelling.

THE CARE/HARM ETHICAL ZONE AND ETHICS

AS I REFLECT on the numerous books that I have read about ethics, it now strikes me that what they mostly say is businesses need to stop focusing so much about money (the Ethical Zone of Rationality and Reason in the next chapter) and care more about people (the Care/Harm Ethical Zone). One manifestation of this is the Conscious Capitalism organization, which places at its core a higher purpose. Another appearance of this phenomenon is a new form of corporations called benefit corporations (US) or community interest corporations (UK). Benefit corporations are companies dedicated to a "triple bottom line" of "people, planet, and profit," and they have become some of the fastest growing companies in the United States, such as Warby-Parker, Etsy, and Stonyfield Organic.

Some businesses have the Care/Harm Ethical Zone at their foundation, like health care. After all, what is the core of health care except caring for people? An example is St. Joseph's Aspirin, which has incorporated a heart into its logo and used the line "put a little love in your heart." (Note: Although heart in the logo does accurately connote the use of the product to prevent heart attacks, the love in the phrase takes it a step further, clearly into the Care/Harm Ethical Zone.) I believe that having the Care/Harm Ethical Zone at the core of your business holds you to a higher standard than other businesses. (I will explore this more in a later chapter.)

The toy industry is another that has the Care/Harm Ethical Zone at its core—Care for children. Children particularly need Care from adults, which makes it a powerful association. Violation of this zone will cause an uproar, for example, if it is discovered that a toy hurts a child either literally (toys that children can swallow, for example) or even hypothetically (toys that collect data that can be used against the child in the future). Care for the children must be at the core of any toy business. If not, it will run the risk of alienating its customers. (Full disclosure: I used to work for a toy company and on advertising for children's cereal before my work in pharmaceuticals.)

Many businesses popular with millennials, such as TOMS shoes—which gives away a pair of shoes for every pair you buy—have used the Ethical Zone of Care/Harm for its branding, even though it isn't at the core of the business.

The origin story of TOMS illustrates how they came to add the Care/Harm Zone. TOMS was founded when Blake Mycoskie (no, his name isn't Tom) was traveling in Argentina and saw the effect that giving a pair of shoes had on a child. Suddenly, children's lives were changed. Two brothers who were sharing one pair of shoes that was too large and alternating going to school (because the school required shoes) could now both go to school. Mycoskie had the thought to not just give the shoes away, but rather to sell shoes on the premise that for every shoe you buy, the company would give a pair to a needy child.

The business took off, growing three-hundred-percent a year for the first five years, becoming a hit with millennials. Mycoskie is quite clear on what the corporate social mission does for TOMS: "It allows us to build an emotional bond with customers and motivate employees, because they know they are shopping and working for a movement bigger than themselves." This is the emotional branding that the Care/Harm Ethical Zone can create.

Building a business is work and creating a process that makes a business run well is a slog. Mycoskie found himself running out of steam.

Taking a long honeymoon, he found himself energized when he read Simon Sinek's work and rediscovered the *why* behind the formation of the business. In his words: "The 'why' of TOMS—using business to improve lives—is bigger than myself, the shoes we sell, or any future products we might launch." For him to remain energized about the why, he felt the need to expand beyond shoes, and started to sell coffee and now other products as well.

The success of TOMS has spawned a movement, now called social enterprise, which seeks adding social value to differentiate the company from its competitors. Besides TOMS and Warby Parker's eyeglasses, many companies are giving away their products such as Bombas, Everything Happy, Hand in Hand Soap, WeWood, and Headbands of Hope. I found a list of thirty-five such companies at https://influencedigest.com/business/top-35-socially-conscious-companies-that-give-back/. I am sure there are many more. During one season on *Shark Tank*, it seemed as if every third company was trying to use the "buy one, give one" business model.

Simon Sinek argues that one can build and sustain these movements only when leading with the why. People follow you, buy from you, when they believe what you believe. I would argue that because you need to stay in touch with the Ethical Zone of Care/Harm.

Using the Ethical Zone of Care/Harm to emotionally brand does work. A Korean social enterprise has been demonstrated to have "a positive effect on trust, reputation, and brand equity."

Sometimes the "borrowed interest" of the Ethical Zone of Care/Harm can be even further from the core of the business. While the decision to donate shoes is a relatively strong connection because TOMS sells shoes, Mycoskie's decision to donate products such as coffee pulls it further away because TOMS doesn't sell coffee. TOMS recent endorsement of gun-control is an even weaker connection. Other weak connections are when your drugstore or grocery asks you to donate to world hunger or when it sponsors a breast cancer race or when the hotel chain offers to donate to a hunger charity if you book with them directly instead of a third party (see the Omni Hotels' Goodnight to Hunger campaign).

Similarly, for decades, United Colors of Benetton used their ad campaigns that put a face on humanitarian issues to emotionally brand with the Care/Harm Ethical Zone. That has backfired recently in a marketing landmine, as a different business owned by the Benetton family has been discovered to be the corporate entity behind the 2018 tragic bridge collapse in Genoa, Italy, that killed at least thirty-five people. A few years earlier, they ran into a different Care/Harm-related marketing landmine when it was discovered that Benetton clothes were being made in the garment factory in Bangladesh that collapsed, which is a tighter connection to the core business than the collapse of the bridge. If you use the Care/Harm Ethical Zone to emotionally brand, your company needs to be squeaky clean.

If, instead of taking on a random humanitarian issue, Benetton had worked toward helping employees of their contractors, the effort might have had a more substantial impact on the company and its target audience because it would have been more tightly connected.

Besides the potential of your company's dirty laundry undercutting the emotional branding, such in the Benetton example, raising awareness of, it also opens your company up to charges of greenwashing/pinkwashing. People who are extremely high on the Care/Harm and Fairness Ethical Zones have built-in bullshit detectors. If you don't really mean it, if it isn't a key part of your business, if your message is perceived to be a marketing ploy, or if you are twisting it to your advantage, your branding efforts can do harm in the long run. Attempts like this can backfire with a negative storm of public opinion, and you can be perceived as having co-opted the Care/Harm Ethical Zone.

Critics have made accusations of greenwashing/pinkwashing against shale drill bit companies donating to Susan B. Komen (breast cancer foundation) to paint their drill bits pink; against Allergan using an Indian tribe to shield a product from generic competition; and, most notoriously, the Pepsi commercial with Kylie Jenner offering a Pepsi to protestors from a look-alike Black Lives Matter march. Even the Nike Colin Kaepernick campaign, which overall seems to be well received by Liberals, gets a footnote mention that of course this is to help Nike make money. Kaepernick counteracted those suspicions by donating his fees to charity; Nike didn't.

One blogger felt a need to cross-examine someone at Tom's of Maine after she found out that it was owned by Colgate. She tried to determine for herself whether Colgate had changed the company or whether the Tom's of Maine name was being used to greenwash Colgate. Although she was personally convinced, her blog post sounds defensive about the fact that she is still using Tom's toothpaste even though it is owned by Colgate.

CULTURAL ASPECTS

CARE/HARM IS STRONGEST in the WEIRD countries: Western Europe, Australia, and America. Other countries place higher importance on the other Ethical Zones. It's not that Care/Harm isn't important to them, it just interacts with the other Ethical Zones. This interaction is what leads to violations of Care/Harm that we Westerners can't imagine, such as women being killed for having violated the Sacredness Ethical Zone when they were raped, female genital mutilation, and others.

Other ethnic groups in the West are lower in the Care/Harm Ethical Zone than Liberals, but that is not often recognized. The local director who embezzled from the African hospital was lower in the Care/Harm Ethical Zone (for the patients) than he was for the Belonging Ethical Zone.

CONSOLIDATING WHAT WE LEARNED

THE CARE/HARM ETHICAL Zone is at the core of what most people mean when they think of ethics. It is extremely high among Liberals, and moderately high among Conservatives. But it looks different among the two groups. Among Conservatives it is mediated by three Ethical Zones (Belonging, Authority, and Sacredness). Among Liberals, it mostly interacts with Fairness.

The Care/Harm Ethical Zone is based on reactions in the amygdala and is influenced by levels of two hormones, testosterone and oxytocin. Some products have strong ties to the Care/Harm Ethical Zone, such as pharmaceuticals or toys. The risk of being a business based in the Care/Harm zone is that it holds businesses to a higher standard, opening it up to criticism that doesn't occur with other businesses. Alternatively, some businesses use Care/Harm as borrowed interest in their emotional branding. That borrowed interest can be more closely tied to the purpose of the business (like the businesses that give away their product) or can be more loosely tied (like collecting donations for a worthy cause or using images in their advertising). The risks of borrowed interest in branding are that your company needs to squeaky clean; adverse events can undercut the benefits and cause marketing landmines (like the bridge collapse for Benetton). The potential charge of greenwashing/pinkwashing represents another risk.

The Care/Harm Ethical Zone explodes our hearts, creating an opportunity for emotional branding, but also has the potential to plant a marketing landmine if it is violated. This risk is highest among Liberal target audiences.

CHAPTER 6

THE DMZ: RATIONALITY AND REASON

H UMANS ARE RATIONAL, aren't they? Economists still use a "homo economicus" who makes rational choices in their econometric models even today, but Daniel Kahneman, Amos Tversky, and Richard Thaler (and many others) have upended that conclusion with their extensive work in cognitive psychology and behavioral economics.

Moral Foundations theory created by Jonathan Haidt (and collaborators), which asserts that our reactions depend on Moral Foundations, represents another way in which the assumption of rationality is violated. When people act out of one of what I call Ethical Zones, it seems to others that their actions don't make sense, which is what psychologists love to study. But sometimes people do make choices that make sense on a rational basis.

Here is the completed Ethical Frames model, which adds Rationality and Reason:

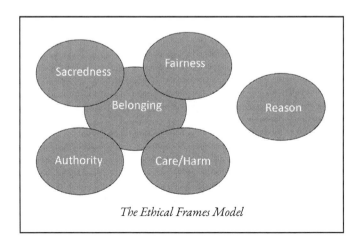

The Ethical Frames Model

I've put Reason outside of the previously discussed zones because it works differently. Even though it can outvote the others, it isn't as emotionally laden as the others. Let's dig into it in more detail.

Take these examples of how, when the Rationality and Reason benefits of either money or convenience bump up against another Ethical Zone, rationality sometimes wins:

- A boarded-up store in rural Georgia with a sign out front "American Owned and Operated" promoted Belonging and Community, which wasn't enough to keep them operating.
- Just a few miles away, the parking lot at Walmart is packed, leading to the closures of small stores in rural areas (like the one just mentioned) because Walmart has lower prices despite their strong Belonging and Community Ethical Zone.
- On the other end of the political spectrum, a hip, urban fair-trade clothing store in Cincinnati struggles to make sales, when even as those who believe in that cause shop at stores where the clothes are cheaper but are made in sweatshops.
- Environmentalists who march for climate change but who let their need for convenience trump that by getting restaurant takeout in containers that contribute to excess waste in landfills or let their family's need overcome their beliefs in climate change by buying an SUV.

An article in the *New York Times* entitled "The Tyranny of Convenience" points out the degree to which we allow convenience to dictate our choices. I would add that financial reasons are also a driver.

You could be judgmental and say that these people aren't acting on their beliefs, as one set of academics did in their book, *The Myth of the Ethical Consumer.* Or you could interpret these pieces of data that when there is a conflict between the Ethical Zone of Rationality and Reason and the other Ethical Zones, the trade-offs that people make vary. Sometimes they will act on the more instinctual Ethical Zone, and sometimes they will choose the most rational choice. Academic research into this issue calls it an intention-behavior gap.

Sometimes the rational doesn't win and facts don't persuade. For example, Conservatives who know the most about climate change are the most against it. Psychologists call this motivated reasoning, when we pick and choose facts to support what we already believe.

In a survey, I created statements to test how many people rely on their Rational Ethical zone on attitudes about the pharmaceutical industry, instead of their Care/Harm and Fairness Ethical Zones. Agreement with the rationality-related Ethical Zone statements was much lower (ranging from ten- to twenty-seven-percent) than statements reflecting either Care/Harm or Fairness (both over sixty-percent). Thus, at least in the context of a market research study, rationality seems to be less of a driver about attitudes toward pharmaceutical companies than the other zones.

BUSINESSES RELY ON RATIONALITY TO MAKE DECISIONS

STEVEN PINKER ENDORSES the idea that societies have been evolving toward greater rationality. I ran across the concept of the rational winning in the long run over the other Ethical Zones at the end of his lengthy tome about violence, *Better Angels of Our Nature*. In it, he pulls together Moral Foundations theory with theories by two anthropologists (Alan Fiske and Richard Shweder) and creates a case for the idea that we, as a society, have been evolving where we use reason more and more. Fiske has tied the development of rationality to the increase in population; operating in larger societies requires different skills.

Pinker applies the idea of rationality to violence, concluding that the increased use of reason has caused a decrease in violence, because reason gives more ways to solve problems. In his view, commerce has been a major source of the greater use of reason. To survive in modern society, you need skills based in reason to accomplish tasks such as calculating the price of things and deciding which is a better deal.

I think he is right. When we create and run businesses, we use money and we make decisions in ways that make sense financially, and we learn to ignore our intuitive Ethical Zones because they don't work as well in that context. When businesspeople ignore the other Ethical Zones, they become hardened to crucial facts about our humanity, and to the fact that others are evaluating their decisions and our actions in terms of the human Ethical Zones they touch, and not just in terms of money.

An illustration of the Ethical Frames model that represents how businesspeople look at issues might look like this, with reason much larger than the others.

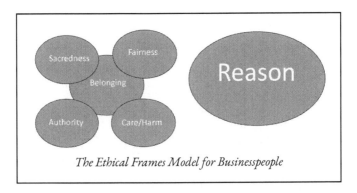

The Ethical Frames Model for Businesspeople

That is very different than the previous versions. In normal society, people who only use Reason and don't use the Care/Harm zone are called psychopaths. Similarly, when businesspeople only use Reason, they are often considered to be psychopathic.

What is behind the difference? Business decisions demand detachment. Business requires analysis. Decisions must make sense financially. A different part of the brain is used in analysis (the frontal cortex), so it's not surprising that people (even if they have empathy in other parts of their lives) don't use their amygdala to make business decisions. Even if you are going to lose money if you don't raise prices, it doesn't matter to the public at large because they aren't using their frontal cortex the way you are. They are using their amygdala, and the amygdala *can't count*.

In Pinker's latest book, *Enlightenment Now*, he again tries to create a case that we should use rational thinking but recognizes that that isn't enough. He proposes that we increase our use of compassion, which is part of the Care/Harm Ethical Zone. I think he is onto something, but I would broaden it to include that those in business need to become aware of and sensitive to *all* the Ethical Zones. They are all real, they all have been evolutionarily useful, and they also have benefits to society today. They are also physiologically based, so we can't change them. When we don't consider these Ethical Zones, we are judging others and being condescending. Instead, we should respect them, try to understand them and collaborate with them where they are and incorporate them into our decisions.

To illustrate how the difference plays out in business versus broader society, consider that eighty-two-percent of the public believes it is unethical to raise prices after a hurricane, but only twenty-four-percent of MBA students do. In evaluating this scenario, consumers are using their instinctual Fairness Ethical Zone; business people are using their Rationality and Reason Ethical Zone. Until business people learn to be aware of the Ethical Zones and how they work, they will keep running into disconnects like these, which can lead to marketing landmines.

Businesses have prided themselves on staying out of politics and of being neutral and of being rational. But the ability to be neutral is diminishing as the country (and perhaps the world) becomes more polarized. In fact, businesses may not realize how affected they are by political polarization. Media decisions are just one of the potential marketing landmines referenced in the title. These decisions can have long-term consequences, which is why you need to learn to make them work for your brand.

Further, marketers have already learned that facts don't persuade by themselves; they persuade as part of a message that appeals to emotion. It is powerful to use an emotion that matches the Ethical Zones that are strong in their customers. Marketers can't expect their customers to always make rational decisions, but sometimes they do. Marketers can make use of the rational with a message based on an Ethical Zone, but it needs to be used thoughtfully and with respect, as I discuss in my chapter on the Rules of Engagement.

CONSOLIDATING WHAT WE LEARNED

RATIONALITY HAS BEEN associated with the evolution of larger societies and is the basis on which businesses have been built. Steven Pinker makes a case that commerce and rationality have contributed to lower levels of violence in society. Businesspeople are termed psychopaths when they don't consider the Care/Harm Ethical Zone. More than that, businesses need to be able to utilize all the different Ethical Zones of the Ethical Frames model in order to be respectful and not condescending. Businesses can be blindsided when they are caught up with their own analysis and don't understand their consumers' beliefs. If they can learn how to use Ethical Zones to emotionally brand and avoid marketing landmines, they will become more successful.

CHAPTER 7
WHEN LANDMINES ARE TRIGGERED: CONFLICT AND CONTROVERSY

THE IDEAS WE have been reviewing are powerful and they drive much of human behavior. They result in high emotion. The six different Ethical Zones that I described work together. Within any individual they can interact, or they can conflict. The Ethical Zones are also a major source of conflict among people and groups. The source of the conflict is either because of different interpretations or different levels of importance of the zones. That last sentence is probably the most important one in the entire book, so you might want to read it again.

I like looking at conflict because it helps me become more fluent in the Ethical Zones. In conflict, one can see how the various zones interact to yield different results. Conflict clarifies, once you use Ethical Frames to look at it.

Here are some examples of political and social conflicts and an analysis using the Ethical Zone model.

- Abortion is a clear issue of conflict that results from different interpretation and importance between the Zones.

    - Liberals focus on the Care/Harm Ethical Zone for the mother, her other children, and that child when it is born. (This isn't surprising due to Liberals' greater emphasis on Care/Harm.)
    - Conservatives focus on the Ethical Zone of Sacredness—Sacredness of life and the unborn child, which is more important to them than Care/Harm

for the mother. (Reminder: Conservatives place less importance on Care/Harm than Liberals, and for them, it interacts with three other Ethical Zones.) They may be also invoking another dimension of the Ethical Zone of Sacredness: that the mother is impure if she has broken the norms of society and had sex outside of marriage. Further, it might touch the Ethical Zone of Fairness: that the woman has sinned and so deserves to be punished. Additionally, the Ethical Zone of Authority may be involved: that she has gone against what authority figures have told her.

- A valedictorian at a Christian high school where her father is on the board is expelled in her senior year because she is pregnant.

    ◦ This is a conflict between the Ethical Zones of Belonging (to the group that she is part of and has been for years) and that of Sacredness (she is impure and might infect the other kids).
    ◦ There could also be another dimension of the Ethical Zone of Sacredness involved: the sanctity of the unborn child. Because she has decided to go through with the pregnancy, she could have been honored for her decision but instead the infection of others dominates. This is consistent with infection as a key motivator of the Sacredness Ethical Zone.
    ◦ There is also an Ethical Zone of Authority involved (the church and her father told her not to have sex, so she has violated that zone) so she deserves to be punished (the Ethical Zone of Fairness).
    ◦ These zones are in play because the school is Conservative. Conservatives place more importance on these three Ethical Zones than Liberals do. It would be very different if it was a Liberal school. For them, the issues would be Care/Harm (the Care of a

young woman at a vulnerable point in her life who made a mistake and Care/Harm for the child when he or she grows up) and Fairness (The young woman is only getting this punishment because she got caught but what about the young man?).

- The children of immigrants being taken away from their parent(s) at the border also presents conflicts among the different zones.

  ◦ For Conservatives, it reflects a conflict between the Ethical Zones of Care/Harm (children awaken a deep desire to Care for them) and of Sacredness (the family is Sacred and so are little children). This issue also awakens the Ethical Zones of Respect for Authority (they aren't in this country legally, they broke the law and should be punished) and of Belonging (they aren't Americans).

    ▪ For some Conservatives, rule of law is paramount.
    ▪ For others, their strong Belonging Ethical Zone kicks in, and the fact that they aren't Americans tamps down their reactions to the Ethical Zones of Care/Harm and Sacredness of the family.
    ▪ But for Conservative women, who have a stronger Care/Harm Ethical Zone, this represents a major conflict.

  ◦ For Liberals, Care/Harm also comes into play but much more strongly because it is so much more important for them. News media that are Liberal focus on the trauma that the separations have caused. Liberals don't have as high a level of importance for the Ethical Zones of Respect for Authority and Sacredness, so that doesn't come for

Liberals on this issue. Instead, another matter comes up, the equality-flavor of the Fairness Ethical Zone. Because those who are the most Liberal believe that those crossing the border have less advantages than we do and we should treat them with even more Care, the need-flavor of the Ethical Zone of Fairness can also come up.

And as stated in the last chapter, rationality can conflict with any of the other zones. The decisions people make signals the relative importance they place on the various Ethical Zones.

CHAPTER 8

THE ARMIES: CONSERVATIVES VS. LIBERALS

S O FAR, WE have learned that all humans have the same Ethical Zones, that some of them are evolutionarily based, and that our conflicts are often based on different interpretations and different importance levels of those Ethical Zones. Here is the Ethical Frames model of the six Ethical Zones that you have seen before that describes how they interact.

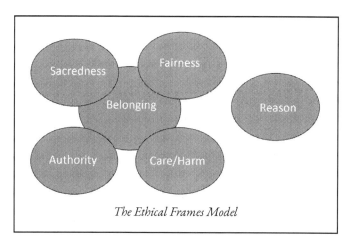

The Ethical Frames Model

A few facts about the world of Liberals and Conservatives to keep in mind as you read this book. The percentage of the US population who consider themselves Conservative is larger than those who are Liberals. In 2017, thirty five percent of adults considered themselves Conservatives versus twenty-six-percent Liberal. The lead Conservatives have over Liberals is declining. That isn't because the Conservative base is shrinking. Instead, Liberals are growing because moderates are becoming more Liberal.

Geographically, Conservatives are located more often in areas with less dense populations and more in the middle of the country than on the coasts. Demographically, Conservatives are more likely older and more likely men with lower levels of education. There is also a difference in occupation. Liberals are more likely to be in jobs that require an advanced education or in a dense population (such as cab drivers) while Conservatives hold jobs that are not tied to education and/or require more open space (such as oil workers.) Even doctor specialty varies: Conservatives are more likely to be primary care doctors, while infectious disease specialists are more likely to be Liberal.

The book *Makers and Takers* by Peter Schweizer summarizes data on Conservatives versus Liberals. According to his sources, Conservatives are

- More satisfied with their lives, their professions, and their health
- More successful parents on average
- More generous
- Less likely to become angry and seek revenge.

However, it should be noted that the word Conservative has been recently recognized to be imprecise. I ran into this at my first presentation on this topic, when a "Conservative" member of the audience got upset at what I was saying. I came to understand that he was upset because there are two different types of Conservatives: social Conservatives and economic Conservatives. Political science research has documented this. Social Conservatives are the larger of the two, so their data dominate the research. Even though this term is imprecise, I'll continue to use because, until recently, all the data have been collected using it. Going forward, there may be some other ways to be more specific, which I will discuss in the chapter on measuring the Ethical Zones. If you are reading this and consider yourself a Conservative, but don't agree with the data on Conservatives, you are probably an economic Conservative.

Throughout most of the book, I have referenced that Conservatives and Liberals place different importance on the Ethical Zones. Instead of the previous graphics of the model where the Ethical Zones are all evenly sized and spaced, I would claim that the Ethical Zones among Conservatives look more like the following diagram, with Belonging sized larger than the others. Note how Fairness and Care/Harm and Sacredness and Authority are equally sized, reflecting their relatively equal importance. Also note how interrelated each of the original five Ethical Zones overlap with Belonging. But not Reason.

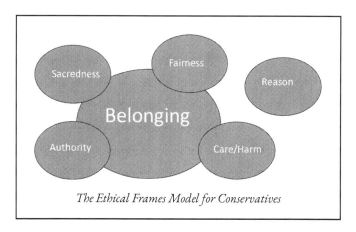

The Ethical Frames Model for Conservatives

In contrast, Ethical Zones for Liberals would look much different. In the next diagram, you see that Fairness and Care/Harm are the largest, overwhelming Belonging, which is smaller but still exists. Sacredness and Authority are still there, but smaller than for Conservatives.

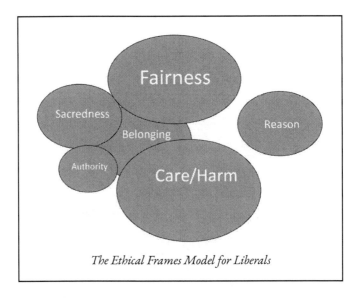

The Ethical Frames Model for Liberals

According to Schweizer's data, Liberals are

- More likely to take care of themselves first and less likely to care for others
- More focused on money
- More interested in leisure than in work
- More prone to depression and nervous breakdown
- More likely to be dishonest
- Less knowledgeable about civic affairs
- More likely to be anxious.

Keep in mind that these are all averages and skews. There are many individual variations that I mentioned, such as variations on how important the Sacredness Ethical Zone is.

There are marketing landmines planted by both armies, but they are different. The landmines for Conservatives are for the Belonging, Authority, and Sacredness Ethical Zones, while the Liberals react to violations of the Care/Harm and Fairness Ethical Zones. And Reason can often act as a demilitarized zone, a place where people can join.

There are also opportunities to harness the emotions behind these armies, to use them in the next generation of emotional branding, Reframing.

CHAPTER 9
RECONNAISSANCE I: DEEP DIVE INTO CONSERVATIVES

I F YOU ARE a Liberal, you have probably been reading news coverage about those who supported President Trump and thinking, how could they say those things? It's easy to dismiss them as prejudiced folks who are dying out.

Keep in mind that the news media go for the extremes, not the average or middle. One estimate is that the segment of "Devoted Conservatives" represent six-percent of the population. Another nineteen-percent are "Traditional Conservatives" while fifteen-percent are "Moderates" who may hold some Conservative values.

It's easy to write a caricature of Conservatives, based on the media coverage of Trump supporters. What's harder is to write a sympathetic profile.

Conservatives value what they have right now and what they had in the past. Keeping order is important to them. They are more conscientious (on average.)

Let's do a reconnaissance into the life of a Conservative. Note that this is a social Conservative, not an economic Conservative. As you read this, try to figure out what you like about these people and what kind of impact they have on the people around them and their world. And listen for what makes them erupt.

Rick is fifty-six years old and served in the army in the Gulf War. He lives in a small town in the Midwest and works on the assembly line in a plant that makes automotive parts. He is married with two kids. His son is in the army, stationed in Afghanistan. His daughter is a junior in high school and considering training to become a nurse. When their kids were young, his wife stayed at home with their two kids, but now works as a receptionist in a legal office.

IN HIS WORDS: I was born and raised in this town and this is where I intend to die. I do what I can to help out here. My daddy and grand-daddy worked real hard to make this town a great place to live, and I do my part. It's tough to see the people moving away and not caring what happens to their hometown. The Walmart moved in thirty years ago, and that killed the downtown. People I know lost their livelihoods when that happened, but that Walmart has more stuff and is cheaper, so you can't fight it. I shop there, and so do they, in fact, some of them work there. But those storefronts are still empty, it's real sad.

I am on the Board of Trustees at the church downtown. The pastor is a real hell-fire-and-damnation preacher, just like we had when I was growing up. He sets a high standard for behavior. He makes sure we know what the right thing to do is. I tithe ten-percent of my income to support it. My old homeroom teacher, Miss Adelia, and her sister, Miss Leila, need my help to be able to stay in their home; otherwise, they would have to go into one of those nursing homes. I do what I can for her. I use my pickup truck to haul stuff for her. My whole family got involved, my wife picked out new shrubs to replace the overgrown ones at the house, and my son helped me dig them out when he was home on leave. My niece goes over there to sit with them and do indoor chores.

My neighbor down the street, Julie, has a son who is one of them homos. He left after high school and went to Chicago. He's the same age as my Sam and was always kind of weird growing up. Didn't want to be on the baseball team and was in the school plays. He got teased a lot then. He's grown up and does something in fashion now, has done real well for himself. I am not in favor of the gay lifestyle—having sex in those baths sounds disgusting—but I have met his "husband" when they came back to visit Julie and he seems real nice. Even though he is gay, Julie's son came from here, so he's one of us. I guess it's better for them to be mar-ried than having sex with lots of people, so I am okay with gay marriage. Now they are talking about adopting an orphan. Family is important.

The work I do is tough, but I am still able to do my part. I am on my feet all day, so I need good work boots. Every Friday, me and my buddies from the plant go out to Joe's for a couple of beers and a game or two of pool—sometimes we shoot darts.

I am concerned that the big bosses will close down the factory and move our jobs to Mexico or China or somewhere else. There's nothing else around, so if that happens, I'm in trouble. I've heard that if they do that, they would give us money to "retrain" but for what? I don't want one of them desk jobs. I didn't like school and I don't like to sit still. The job I have suits me just fine. I can't see moving away to get another job. I've lived here my whole life, and all my family and friends are here. My wife is working, so if that happens, we will get by. I can't imagine not being here. Some of my buddies have tried working on the oil fields because they could make a bunch of money, but they got too lonely and came back.

My buddy Jim got hurt on the line and started taking them opioids and now he's addicted. Just like my buddies from the army, he's one of us, so when he can't make it to work, we guys fill in for him. The line manager knows but he doesn't tell the big shots from out of town. They wouldn't understand. They don't know what it is like to work the line and need your paycheck. I know we can't protect him forever, so I hope he shakes it off real soon before the suits find out. They might make him go to rehab.

Prejudice: I know those Liberals think people like me are prejudiced but I am really not. I have a buddy at work who is black, and I also work with a couple of immigrants. They pull their weight, so they are okay. I just am concerned about our way of life being taken over by people who aren't like us. Why don't they make their own country better rather than come here and ruin ours?

My son is in the army, just like his dad and his granddad. We have a family tradition of supporting our country. He's on his second tour of Afghanistan. I worry what he will do when he gets out of the army, there's not much here for young people to do, especially if the factory closes down. He's married, with two kids, and another one on the way. We do everything we can for our daughter-in-law and our grandkids. My daughter wants to be a nurse. That's okay, I am just worried about her going away to college and learning to not respect our family's values.

Politics: Like the guys I work with, I voted for President Trump. He's the first politician I know of who does get us. Plus, he's rich and successful, so he knows how the world works. I don't spend time reading about the "issues." If the president says what he is doing is the best, I trust him.

On Liberals: Those bleeding-heart Liberals want to ruin the country. They think it doesn't matter if we bring a bunch of immigrants into this country. We have to beat them or else they will destroy everything I love about this country.

Travel: My parents went on a cruise to Bermuda last year. Now that they are retired, they are talking about going to Europe. They will go on one of the tours so that they can be sure to understand everything and won't get lost. That doesn't interest me. Once a year, I take my family on road trips in our RV to see the western part of our beautiful country. We usually go to a national park, but we stay off-site in private campgrounds because they have good bathrooms and showers. For my other vacation, I go fishing or hunting with my buddies.

Food: My wife works, but she gets home in time to make dinner every night, and we have dinner together as a family. She is a great cook. She has a regular schedule that she follows so that I know exactly what will be on the table each night, like Monday night being meatloaf night. We go out to eat once a week, usually to the diner. I always get the same thing, but sometimes we'll go out somewhere else when my son is home.

Abuse: I hear about the sex abuse going on; the women who say they were assaulted by Harvey Weinstein shouldn't have put themselves in that position. If they didn't put themselves in that position, he wouldn't have been able to do that. I like the way Mike Pence handles it, he keeps himself from being in that position. But the stuff with Catholic priests and kids, that's sick and disgusting. It's kids, that's what makes it so bad, they are so innocent. They didn't do anything to deserve that.

NOTE THE LOYALTY to the various groups that he belongs to: his former school teacher and her sister, his coworkers and his line manager, his neighbors, his army buddies. He is also loyal to his community. He served in the armed forces and now his son does. If we didn't have people like Rick and his son, the US wouldn't have as strong an armed force as it does. We need to honor him and his family (Belonging and Community).

Note also his willingness to follow directions if the line manager says so, his support of his hell-fire-and-damnation minister, and his trust of President Trump (Respect for Authority). Note that he isn't interested in more information, he has a high need for cognitive closure.

Note the earning of Fairness—the ethnic coworkers, the women who got abused didn't deserve sympathy because of their bad choices, but the kids were innocent and didn't deserve it (Fairness).

Note the desire for orderliness in all aspects of his life (same dinner on Mondays) and his disgust at homosexual sex and the priests violating children (Sacredness).

Note the commitment he has to making the world a better place and that he actually does do something in his little corner.

Note that he has changed his mind about something (homosexual marriage), and that change is related to a different way of looking at things. He is reflecting the success of the technique of reframing, which I will discuss later. Also note that he is so against the Liberal agenda that he is unlikely to listen to a Liberal argument; instead he is focused on winning the argument.

IN HIS WIFE'S (Ellie) voice:

Rick is pretty worked up about what Liberals are doing to this country. I'm more "live and let live." Liberals have raised some good points, but they get a little extreme. I don't like the way President Trump acts, especially the stuff that he tweets, and the separation of kids from their parents at the border breaks my heart.

My family comes first in my life. I am grateful that Rick was able to make enough money so that I could stay home to raise my kids when they were young. I did go back to work later when they were old enough to be involved in after school activities. My job is in town and flexible. When my kids were younger, they allowed me to come in later, so I could be homeroom mom when my daughter was in middle school. This town is a great place to raise kids; if for some reason I couldn't be there, there are many other people who would step in and help out. My kids each have a group of friends they grew up with and are really close to and can rely on.

I met Rick when he was in the army and moved here when he got out, so I am not from here. I grew up in a suburb of Chicago, so this is different. Sometimes I feel like I will never truly belong, most everyone has lived here their entire lives, and their parents and grandparents too. That's not quite true, I am very involved with stuff here and have made some good friends.

The church is a big part of our lives; Rick is on the trustees, and our social life revolves around it. I am part of the church women's group and the couples club at church does a progressive dinner every month. The minister has some definite ideas about what is right and I listen closely to what he says because he has studied the Bible.

I try to have dinner on the table every night when Rick comes home. He likes to eat the same thing every week, so we have meal/day pairings like meatloaf Mondays and fish Fridays. I like to try something new once in a while, and as long as I don't do it too often, he won't complain.

I hope my kids have as good a life as Rick and I did. My oldest is in the army, and I am really proud of him. Caitlyn wants to be a nurse and help people. I want to do everything I can to support her. I am a little concerned about where she wants to go study nursing, but I grew up in the suburbs and I turned out okay, so I am not as scared the way Rick is.

NOTE HOW ELLIE is more moderate than Rick, which is a typical gender difference. Ellie is more concerned about family (both the Care/Harm and Sacredness Ethical Zones). Despite this, she has made different choices than a more Liberal woman would about raising her family. She had children when she was younger than a Liberal woman, which is typical. Again, Ellie is as involved with organizations and connected to her community even though she moved there as an adult, and doesn't always feel like she fits in. She does pay attention to what authority figures say, but she also works around them, if they say something she disagrees with, such as when she only tries new meals occasionally.

CHAPTER 10
RECONNAISSANCE II: DEEP DIVE INTO LIBERALS

L IBERALS, OR PROGRESSIVES, believe in the goodness of man; they believe that problems that people have are due to the restrictions that society places on them. They take for granted the freedoms and privileges of the society they were raised in and are always looking to improve the society they live in. They have a focus on the new and the novel. They also have a sunnier view about the dangers of life and want their kids to be free to explore and be curious.

Liberals place extremely high importance (much higher than Conservatives) on two Ethical Zones: Care/Harm and Fairness. It's not that Conservatives don't place importance on those two Ethical Zones; it's just Liberals place an extreme importance on them. When you read or listen to news stories from a source that appeals to Liberals, the emphasis is always on how people have been hurt. Fairness is important to both Liberals and Conservatives, but Liberals have a different interpretation. Unlike for Conservatives, whose Fairness flavor is merit, Liberals believe either that everyone deserves the same (the equality-flavor), or that some people deserve more to make up for their disadvantaged history (the need-flavor).

Look at the differences between the Conservative and Liberal profile and ask yourself, who would you prefer to be your neighbor? Who does more to make the world a better place?

Darryl is a forty-nine-year-old IT manager with an insurance company who lives in a big city. He's from the Midwest but went away to college for computer science. There are no IT jobs in the town where he was born, so he has never lived there as an adult, but he visits his parents every couple of years.

He commutes an hour each way to the city, and his wife is a consultant who works out of their suburban home but travels for work. They have two kids, ages ten and eight. Their son, Jonathan, is a geek, while Hayley is into her American Girl dolls. Here are his words:

WHEN LAURA QUIT her job to work at home as a consultant, I thought our life would get a lot easier. Well, it is mostly, except when she is traveling. The more successful she is, the more she travels, and the more stressful our lives become. We hired someone to come to our house to be there when the kids come home and take them to all their activities, but she can't work longer hours when my wife is away. My kids can do a sleepover at their friend's sometimes, but we have to get really creative when she is on a long trip; we have had my mother come in to stay with us a couple of times, and once we had to hire a British-style nanny to come to live with us for two weeks when my wife went to China.

I love that my wife's income allows us to take great vacations. We went to the Turks & Caicos last year for two weeks to relax but, overall, our lives are pretty crazy. We don't eat dinner together very often. Because the kids have so many activities, they aren't home at the same time. And I get home late from work a lot. So everyone just eats when they get hungry. We tried out one of the home-meal kits things, but we don't eat together enough to make it work for us. Plus, the kids are picky eaters, so we let them choose their favorites. We order in pizza a lot. We shop at lot on Amazon and use it even more now that we got an Alexa.

I am under a lot of pressure at work. There's a lot of cyberattacks, and I have to stay up-to-date on the latest software and the latest threats. If something happens, I will probably lose my job. I want to hire an AI specialist, but we can't get a visa to hire someone from abroad. Since I can't find someone here in the US who has the skills I need, I probably can't find someone to help me. I am thinking about looking for another job before this blows up. I am considering whether I should consider jobs outside this area and then either do a long-distance commute or maybe we would have to move.

My department is almost all men, mostly Asian. I have learned to love ethnic food from hanging out with them; they know the best places in the city.

The neighborhood we live in is mostly people about our age; it's a new condo development. It is diverse, with lots of Asians and a few African American families. I don't know much about our town. It's almost like I am really just here to sleep, except when I go to school functions for my kids.

On the weekends, I get together with my buddies and we play squash. I haven't been to church since the last time I went to visit my folks on a holiday. I don't have time to go to church. We do all our errands on the weekends, plus I am not quite sure if I still believe in the God I was taught about as a kid. If God is so powerful, why does God allow all those bad things to happen? Plus, those right-wing pastors give me the willies.

I am really concerned about climate change. I want a world where my kids can enjoy everything the world can offer. I've signed petitions and voted for candidates who want to do something. We bought a hybrid car that I use to go to the station, but it really doesn't fit all four of us and our stuff. We use my wife's SUV for family trips even though it isn't really good for the environment.

Laura's parents are failing, and we don't know what to do. Thank goodness her sister lives near their parents, but it's not fair that she has to do everything. Laura tries to do what she can, but between the kids' schedules and her work and travel and everything, it's not much. Laura doesn't have time to volunteer for the PTO, but she does make cupcakes when asked, if she is in town.

Politics: I voted for Hillary. I don't understand how people can like President Trump, he seems like an idiot. He is racist and incites violence.

On Conservatives: I don't understand the people I grew up with. When I go back to visit my folks, I hear my old high school classmates mouthing off about how immigration is ruining this country. How do they know? They don't have many immigrants in their town, just the doctor who moved there ten years ago. They sound so prejudiced. We don't talk politics with my folks. I don't want to get into a fight.

NOTE HE BELONGS to no groups. It's like where he lives is a hotel. There is nothing he is loyal to, not even the company he works for.

Note how he makes the decisions for his own life, not his manager (low in Respect for Authority). Note the comfort with immigrants (his Belonging is to the world, not his town or his country). Note the chaos and lack of structure in his life (low in Sacredness). Note the Care for others—his wife's parents, the world, the environment but low involvement.

The wife's perspective:

DARRYL IS FROM a small town in Iowa, but I grew up in the suburbs of Chicago. Darryl and I met in college; he majored in computer science and I was a business major. When it came time to look for jobs, we decided to look in a city that I knew, Chicago. It isn't that far from Iowa, so we can drive to see his parents for holidays. We both got good jobs and have been making good money.

We waited to have kids after we got married so I could get established in my career. Boy, did having kids complicate our lives! Don't get me wrong, I love my kids and would do almost anything for them. But juggling my demanding job, the commute, and everything the kids needed was draining. We did hire a nanny, but there still wasn't enough time in the day. So I decided to start a consulting practice, working from home. That has made my life easier, most days, and we did keep the nanny for after school. But when I travel on business, things get hairy. Then we have to patch together a bunch of people chipping in. It's hard because we don't know that many people in the town we live in, but the kids have made friends, and I know their mothers. Luckily, my mother and my sister aren't that far away, so they can fill in too. I hate to rely on Mom, though, because she isn't doing that well.

I try to get involved in my kids' schools. I go to PTA meetings, bring cupcakes, and handled organizing a booth at the school's spring festival. But that is about all I can do and stay sane.

Food is an issue in our house. I am too busy to think about dinner, and the nanny doesn't take care of dinner. I have set up a recurring food order at Amazon using Prime, so the basics are delivered, thank God.

Just like all kids, ours want typical stuff like mac and cheese, but Darryl and I are more adventurous. So we order food delivered from our local restaurants, like the sushi place a few miles away or the latest ethnic restaurant. Often, the kids have already eaten by the time our food comes, so we don't eat together. They need to eat as soon as they get home from their activities, because they are starved.

LAURA WAITED TO have kids, unlike Ellie, which is typical of a Liberal family. Both Laura and Ellie grew up in the suburbs of Chicago, but Ellie has made choices that fit with her move to rural America with her husband, such as having kids earlier, going to church, and getting involved in the community. Laura tries to get involved a little bit, but is exhausted from trying to juggle it all, while Ellie has more time and can handle it more easily. Ellie recognizes that her husband's beliefs are more extreme than hers, while Laura is more in sync with her husband.

CHAPTER 11
STEPPING ON LANDMINES

SINCE I HAVE spent more than two decades in the pharmaceutical industry, I am going to use that experience (and other health-related stories) as examples of how applying the Ethical Frames model can help provide insight into the market.

VACCINATION IN ENGLAND

AS PART OF the work that won him the Nobel Prize in economics, economist Angus Deaton analyzed mortality trends. He found that the introduction of vaccination for smallpox was an important factor in the decrease in deaths in England during the eighteenth century. Because the aristocracy were first to adopt vaccination, their death rate dropped almost a century before the lower classes.

When Dr. Deaton spoke about this at a talk at the Princeton Library in 2016, he was asked for the reasons behind the aristocracy's earlier adoption. He listed several possibilities: It could have been the ability to pay or it might have been other factors, such as trusting the newfangled technology or just knowing someone who had been vaccinated.

The Liberal Princeton audience had a negative emotional reaction to the fact that the lower class didn't have equal access to lifesaving technology, reflecting the Liberal emphasis on the Care/Harm Ethical Zone and the equality-flavor of Fairness. A Conservative audience probably wouldn't have had the same reaction. Remember how much larger the Fairness and Care/Harm Ethical Zones are among Liberals than among Conservatives.

Interestingly, even though Dr. Deaton defended the historical event as reasonable, when he was later asked a question about drug prices, he said they were too high, reflecting the current sensibility of Liberals. Why this difference in his attitude between the past and the present? I didn't ask Dr. Deaton, but I have an idea. In that earlier time, it was common for the lives of commoners to have less value (the merit-flavor of the Fairness Ethical Zone). Further, the emphasis on the Care/Harm Ethical Zone is much higher today than it was then.

I presume that Dr. Deaton was channeling eighteenth-century attitudes in his earlier answer—lower importance on the Ethical Zone of Care/Harm and the merit-flavor of the Fairness Ethical Zone. When he was asked the question about today's drug prices, I think he switched into today's Liberal beliefs, which I will review later.

THE ANTIVACCINE MOVEMENT

THE CURRENT ANTIVACCINE movement represents another opportunity to examine how the Ethical Zone model explains attitudes and behavior. Back in 2000, I did a study about attitudes of parents toward children's vaccines for the Merck vaccine division. One of the main drivers of attitudes toward vaccines were attitudes toward doctors, with one segment named "Trust My Doctor." Those who were *less* likely to vaccinate their kids were low on trusting their doctor.

Although I hadn't developed the Ethical Zone concept back then, in retrospect, those who were antivaccine were likely to be low in Respect for Authority. A later 2018 study that profiled antivaxxers using Moral Foundations theory found that they were likely to be higher in the Sacredness Ethical Zone.

Knowing these two skews in Ethical Zones of antivaxxers is good news because it can help identify ways to address their concerns. Given their lower level of Respect for Authority, efforts that rely on doctors and other Authority figures are not likely to be successful. Later, I will talk about the technique of reframing, which provides some clues on how to convince these mothers who are low in the Ethical Zone of Respect for Authority, but high on the Ethical Zone of Sacredness.

DRUG PRICES

HIGH DRUG PRICES are an emotional minefield. What's interesting to me, as someone who used to work in the pharmaceutical industry, is that the high-profile examples are (mostly) for drugs that have been around for a long time. Two drugs that often mentioned are Daraprim, which had its price raised overnight by seven-hundred-and-fifty-percent by the notorious Martin Shkreli, and the EpiPen, for which Mylan increased the price over five-hundred-percent over seven years. Although it didn't make as much of a splash, a recent article in the *Financial Times* highlighted a CEO who had raised the price of the drug he had purchased by four-hundred-percent and who was quoted as saying he had a "moral requirement" to make money. As I said, these are all drugs that have been around for a long time

Branded drugs, for which companies have invested years of development, are treated differently. While people goggle at the prices of branded drugs which cost a lot of money (the usual threshold is $100,000 per year for that sort of press coverage), it does not elicit the same sort of outrage as the price increases on older drugs. Let's look at drug prices through the lens of the Ethical Frames model to see if we can figure out why they are treated differently.

These data come from a study in early 2018 I did of 400 consumers, half Democrats and half Republicans. (Note: For more details, my publication *Reactions to Drug Prices* can be ordered through my website, www.ethicalframes.com.)

Liberals had higher regard for the pharmaceutical industry on attributes such as "saving lives" and "providing drugs with few side effects" than Conservatives—both consistent with Liberal's greater concern for the Care/Harm Ethical Zone. They also are more likely to recommend development of drugs for rare diseases, even if they were warned that the price would be high. Additionally, they believe that providing free drugs for people who can't afford them is more important than Conservatives do, reflecting their equality-flavor of the Fairness Ethical Zone.

So, Liberals are pharmaceutical industry supporters. Despite this, they got hot under the collar about the idea that pharmaceutical companies "care more about profit than about people," which is another way of saying that Care/Harm should matter more than Rationality and Reason. They are also significantly more likely to say that pharmaceutical companies pay their executives "excessively high salaries" and take "excessive profits"—both statements reflecting the equality-flavor of the Fairness Ethical Zone. Remarkably, these Ethical Zones have affected their beliefs about the facts of the matter: Liberals were more likely (than Conservatives) to believe that the "cost of drugs is much higher in the US than in Canada" and that the "cost of drugs is way too high." Importantly, the degree of emotion and the misperceptions were *not* correlated with having problems paying for their own drugs. Self-interest was not creating landmines; that would be the Ethical Zone of Rationality and Reason. Instead, consumers were reacting in a way that reflected the importance they placed on the Ethical Zones of Care/Harm and Fairness.

Conservatives have their own hot buttons, which aren't as extreme in this case. They are more likely to say that it is important to educate doctors about new drugs and are less likely to say that they will challenge their doctor—both issues reflecting their greater importance on the Authority Ethical Zone. Because of this, it is likely that direct-to-consumer advertising is less effective with Conservatives than it is for Liberals. They are also more likely to agree with a statement that Donald Trump made that drug companies are getting away with murder, again reflecting the greater importance they place on the Authority Ethical Zone.

As might be expected, Conservatives are also higher on attributes that reflect the Belonging Ethical Zone. They are more likely to say that Americans should have faster access and more access to medications than people in other countries, a nationalistic attribute that reflects the stronger Belonging Ethical Zone.

Now that we understand the overall data skews, let's focus on the price increases for Daraprim and the EpiPen. The reactions mirror those noted in the Fairness Ethical Zone chapter, where I cited the data that eighty-two-percent are outraged over an increase in prices of building supplies after a hurricane. When looking at price increases, given Conservatives' greater attachment to the status quo, I expected them to be more resistant to price increases. That wasn't true. Instead it was Liberals who were significantly more likely to say that it is not "Fair" to have large price increases, reflecting their greater Fairness emphasis.

I think that the reason Liberals may not get as upset about high prices for drugs for rare diseases as they do about the price increases for generic drugs is related to a recognition of the effort it takes to develop a drug—merit-flavored Fairness Ethical Zone type of thinking, which is not characteristic, but may apply in this situation. That's why the drugs that generate outrage are old drugs from companies that increase prices a lot, because they haven't *earned* the right to raise the price, just like the retailers didn't earn the right to charge a higher price for goods after a hurricane.

The CEO who said that he had to raise the price four-hundred-percent because he had lost money in buying a plant hadn't earned the right. It was "only" money, it wasn't effort. Similarly, Martin Shkreli's promise to invest the money in development was ignored, or not believed, or just plain didn't matter. The Ethical Zone of Fairness in price justification seems to require effort, not just money.

Allergan's recent sale of its patent for Restasis (an eye drug) to an American Indian tribe also touches on these issues. Allergan was attempting to use the Care/Harm and Fairness Ethical Zones to get around the issues of patent protection. Allergan probably saw this to get Liberals on their side. After all, they were providing for those in need – the need-flavor of Fairness. What they failed to see is that Liberals would view this effort as an attempt to co-opt the Mohawk tribe for monetary reasons—which is a Liberal "crime"! This reaction is similar to that for the Pepsi Black Lives Matter ad. Greenwashing!

Conservatives wouldn't be as upset about this issue, because, for them, the Care/Harm and Fairness Ethical Zones interact with the other zones, such as Belonging and Community and Sacredness. American Indian tribes don't belong to their in-group (that is, the Belonging Ethical Zone), and those who are not like them may violate their Sacredness Ethical Zone as well. Those on the right either might be indifferent to it, or it might even backfire, because that could call into question the purity of the drug.

CHAPTER 12
THE IEDS: THE BIOLOGICAL BASIS OF POLITICAL POLARIZATION

PERSONALITY ATTRIBUTES, BRAIN functioning, and hormones all play a role in creating these emotional improvised explosive devices that are sprinkled throughout the marketing environment. In this chapter, I will review the scientific research that documents that our differences are not just in attitude; they have a deeper origin.

These differences start early; neurons for both children and adults react differently when they see an image of an in-group member versus an out-group member. Infants spend more time looking at faces that are similar to their caregivers. In adulthood, the involuntary responses relating to the Ethical Zone of Belonging and Community affect saliva and sweat production. Conservatives spend more time looking at negative images than Liberals, reflecting their gloomier worldview. Winning generates dopamine, which is the pleasure hormone. These physiological reactions are probably the source of the results that are found in the implicit bias test that demonstrates that many, many people are prejudiced.

Those who are high in Respect for Authority tend to be higher in a desire for orderliness and conscientiousness, which are two of the big five of the attributes that psychologists use describe the fundamental aspects of our personality. Recently, researchers have found that following commands reduces anxiety compared with making your own decisions.

Liberals are more anxious than Conservatives. Conservatives also have higher need for cognitive closure. Liberals have greater responses to the ACC (anterior cingular cortex), which is involved in error detection and resolving conflict. This is may be the cause of Liberals' greater tolerance of ambiguity, lower need for cognitive closure, and lower Respect for Authority.

Conservatives are also more sensitive to disgusting images, which is related to the Sacredness Ethical Zone. Taking an anti-nausea drug has been shown to tamp down disgust reactions, even on non-food related issues.

The Care/Harm Ethical Zone is related to production of two hormones, testosterone and oxytocin, which affect the functioning of the empathy center, the amygdala. Testosterone blocks the amygdala functioning while oxytocin promotes it, which influences the gender skew of politics.

The Rationality and Reason Ethical Zones rely on the frontal cortex, which can compute percentages and make cost comparisons. This is what Daniel Kahneman called System 1 in his work. But System 1 uses lot of energy and is slow, so humans don't use System 1 very often. Businesspeople use System 1 in their work, so they have developed answers based on rational thinking using a totally different part of their brain than the parts their consumers use.

Conflicts are related to the fact that people are using different parts of their brains when they place different importance on the different zones. For example, when Liberals are thinking pro-choice thoughts about abortion, they are probably using the amygdala, the seat of empathy and the Care/Harm Ethical Zone. In contrast, Conservatives may be focused on the Sacredness Ethical Zone when thinking about abortion and using their anterior insula. No wonder we talk past each other!

We are all subject to motivated reasoning. Conservatives and Liberals actually *perceive* data differently, in such a way that supports their current perceptions.

It's not surprising that we can't convince anyone of our point of view when they are using a different part of their brain and when we are asking them to do things that go against their natural tendency. But there is hope. If there is anything marketers are great at, it is working with people where they are.

This is just another way to do that.

The different Ethical Zones that I have been talking about use different parts of our brains and relate to different physiological processes and personality characteristics. That's why we can't talk to each other until we understand our differences.

CHAPTER 13
MAPPING THE MINEFIELD: MEASURING ETHICAL ZONES

THE 2016 ELECTION of Donald Trump was a surprise for most people. Why did this happen? Although the analysis of the polls by the website FiveThirtyEight.com did give a small chance of a win to Donald Trump, the polls also probably undercounted the support for Donald Trump. Some pointed to the shy Trump voter. A similar phenomenon happened during the Brexit vote.

As you have learned in the previous chapters, Conservatives are likely to feel differently than Liberals. They may or may not be willing to say what they feel in front of others who they feel might judge them. They don't like it when people are condescending. In the insights business, we have been so focused on the latest technology that we may be leaving behind a major source of insights that we could get by making these people comfortable. Or it may be that we are tempted to dismiss them as being prejudiced and not take time to understand them.

In order to implement the lessons learned here, you need to first understand what Ethical Zones are most active for the target audience in your category.

The first step is to scan the environment to look for clues that there is an Ethical Zone involved. You can start by mining data that already exist. This could be data you have collected yourself, or data that exist in syndicated services, or data on the web:

- Doing an analysis of verbatims that you have from previously conducted studies using the Ethical Frames vocabulary list (available at www.ethicalframes.com)

- Doing a text analysis of comments people have made on the internet or social media or even the news using that same list
- Seeing what syndicated data already exist about political preferences of your users. One vendor, Connexity, includes this as a data field.

If none of that works, you can add a question or set of questions to any quantitative study you are fielding. Some possible questions are these:

- Use the Liberal versus Conservative scale. (While this scale is easy to use and has been validated, recent research has proven that the scale doesn't differentiate between economic and social Conservatives, who have different profiles. You may wish to modify this scale or use one of the other techniques.)
- The parenting style questions can help identify those who are higher in Respect for Authority.
- The need for cognitive closure questions again identifies those who are higher in Respect for Authority.
- The Moral Foundations Questionnaire (https://moralfoundations.org/questionnaires) is longer than you might want to include in a separate study but is good at identifying those who are Conservative. This could also be used if you want to talk to Liberals who don't fit the overall pattern because they are high in one factor specifically. I am thinking about those Liberals who are high in the Ethical Zone of Sacredness, which could be useful if you are researching the antivaccine movement or the attitudes about GMOs, or if you are operating in a category in which the Sacredness Ethical Zone is operative (such as food, beauty, or cleaning).
- A quick and easy technique that might help identify those who are high in purity is to add "is disgusting" to any attribute battery. Those who rate it the highest are probably the highest in this Ethical Zone.

If you analyze attitudinal questions about your brand by the responses to those questions, you will magnify the differences, and then you can figure out the potential for using Ethical Zones in your segmentation, targeting, and messaging.

Once you have figured out that this might be helpful, you can do a special qualitative project to dig into the Ethical Zones that are operative in your category and for your brand. Key parts to this—

- The groups need to be homogeneous for political preferences; otherwise, some people will not be totally honest. You need to encourage the shy Trump voter to speak. You can use any of the previous methods to recruit homogeneous groups.
- Consider doing groups in second- and third-tier cities, not just in major metros where the majority are Liberals. Online groups might also be a good option, but they don't have the power of in-person groups to create Belonging and make people feel comfortable. You could end up with just the extremes, which isn't a good idea.
- Set everyone at ease and make sure that they know they are among people like themselves.
- Use the Ethical Frames vocabulary list to be able to pick up on and probe on themes. This is available upon request at my website: www.ethicalframes.com.
- Use the Ethical Frames image library (available to clients) to provide more information about how the Ethical Zones are operating in your category and your brand.
- Once you know the Ethical Zones that are most engaged by the groups, have the team write statements that reflect that back to the respondents, and check to make sure you have it correctly.

Combined with an Ethical Zone profile of respondents, those statements can then be used in future quantitative research to discern how widespread the thinking is and the impact that it has on your category and brand. Then you can explore the possibilities for developing emotional branding for your product. They can also be powerful when used as in a segmentation study, especially because it is so easy to use them to target.

CHAPTER 14
IS A CEASE-FIRE POSSIBLE? REFRAMING

ARE YOU DISCOURAGED? It seems overwhelming how different people are and how solidly entrenched those differences are. Don't give up hope. A cease-fire is possible. Lots of people are working on this issue. A number of techniques have been tested and demonstrated to be successful in changing people's minds on an issue,

Because high need for cognitive closure is a core issue, most of these tasks require a big commitment of time and energy, which is exactly what advertisers don't have. I have written a summary of those time-intensive techniques but haven't included it in this book because it is so difficult to do in an advertising setting. (If you are interested, you can request a copy of my summary at www.ethicalframes.com.)

Despite this difficulty, Heineken did produce a four-minute, twenty-five-second video in which they showed had people with opposing views to get to know each other first before revealing their differences. Kudos to Heineken for trying (view the insightful video here:

https://www.youtube.com/watch?v=8wYXw4K0A3g&
oref=https%3A%2F%2Fwww.youtube.com%2Fwatch%3Fv%3D8wYX
w4K0A3g&has_verified=1)

One of the innovative techniques stands out as appropriate for advertising because it doesn't require a large commitment of time: reframing. The premise of reframing is that no issue is *inseparably* tied to an Ethical Zone. Almost every issue can be viewed through a number of different Ethical Zones. Changing the interpretation of the issue by switching Ethical Zones can work to change people's minds on that particular issue. Figuring out how to change the Ethical Zone that is associated with an issue is tricky, but it can be done. A key factor is that you need to use an Ethical Zone that is strong for the target audience, is relevant to the issue, but is not currently used to support the issue.

Academic reframing experts Robb Willer and Matt Feinberg have done a number of studies demonstrating that it can be done. They used the technique on five different societal issues:

- Increased military spending was supported by more Liberals when framed using the need-based flavor of Fairness (that the military increases opportunities for the disadvantaged populations who are more likely to be in the military) than when it was framed using Belonging, a Conservative Ethical Zone.
- Universal health care was supported by significantly more Conservatives when the Sacredness Ethical Zone (sick people are disgusting) was used than when an equality-flavored Fairness Ethical Zone argument was used.
- Same-sex marriage was supported by more Conservatives when it was framed using Belonging-based arguments than when it was framed using Fairness arguments and more than when it was not framed at all.
- Liberals were more likely to support making English the official language of the US when it was framed as a Fairness issue than when it was framed as a Belonging issue.
- Conservatives were more likely to support environmental issues when they were framed using the Sacredness Ethical Zone than when they supported using the Care/Harm Ethical Zone.

Robb Willer's excellent TEDxMarin talk on reframing can be found at https://www.ted.com/talks/robb_willer_how_to_have_better_political_conversations.

I have found several examples of successful reframing in the real world:

- The Texas anti-littering campaign is the premier example of using the Belonging and Community Ethical Zone. It has run for thirty years and had been effective in decreasing littering in Texas. In it, they tie not littering with being a Texan. They have a website (http://www.dontmesswithtexas.org/) where you can see the various iterations of the successful campaign.

- A campaign for recycling in Conservative Utah that I discovered on a trip to Utah may have been created by someone familiar with Willer and Feinberg's work. It uses the Ethical Zone of Sacredness, just like one of the Willer/Feinberg studies.

- A century ago life insurance was regarded as disgusting because it was associated with death (a prime example of violating the Sacredness Ethical Zone) but has been reframed to be about caring for your family after you are gone (using the Care/Harm Ethical Zone), which has totally changed customers' reactions.

- As illustrated in the Deep Dive into Conservatives chapter, it may be that the acceptance of gay marriage has changed because the issue moved from the Care/Harm and Fairness Ethical Zones favored by Liberals (people deserve to love who they wish) to one that touched on a Conservative hot button, the family, which touches both the Belonging and Sacredness Ethical Zones (Gays should be able to marry and form families.). This reframing also avoids the negative Sacredness of people have multiple sex partners.

- A story I heard from someone about a small town in upstate New York illustrates how Belonging can be reframed. The town held a beauty contest in which a young Muslim girl had enrolled, but she couldn't participate in the swimsuit portion of the contest because of her religion. Although the Belonging and Sacredness Ethical Zones could have easily lead to her rejection because of prejudice, that didn't happen. Instead, the town rallied around her and allowed her to participate because "she's one of us." It's amazing how flexible the Belonging and Community Ethical Zone can be; her Muslim "otherness" could have been used against her, but it wasn't. Instead, she was embraced as one of the Community.

- There is an attempt to get firefighters to wear protective masks, which goes against the macho firefighter culture (a Belonging Ethical Zone). The reframing is using the phrase "clean is the new cool," which invokes the Sacredness Ethical Zone.
- A pro-life campaign, "Real Men Love Babies," attempts to redefine masculinity using the Belonging Ethical Zone, instead of the Ethical Zone that is usually invoked, Care/Harm.

A podcast that discussed Spiral Dynamics gives other examples of using reframing for car sales, which can be found here:

http://www.theliturgists.com/podcast/2014/9/23/episode-5-spiral-dynamics

Here is my interpretation:

- If you were a car salesperson going to sell a car to someone for whom the Belonging and Community Ethical Zone was highly active, it would be compelling to say that people like you, from the group you belong to, are buying this car.
- For a person in whom the Respect for Authority is highly active, saying that an authority figure has said that this is a good car is a compelling message.
- If the Sacredness Ethical Zone is crucial, then you might want to emphasize the safety of the vehicle or that it can take your family to church.
- Saying you deserve the car can activate the merit-flavor of the Fairness Ethical Zone.
- If the person is strong in the Care/Harm Ethical Zone, you may want to emphasize safety but with an emphasis on the kids.
- Finally, for the person in whom the Rational is dominant, you would want to emphasize features like the gas mileage and low maintenance costs or the ease of parking or how good a deal you can get.

This sounds promising! But there's a caution. When Willer and Feinberg asked research participants to create an ethically based argument that would persuade the other side, most people didn't. They couldn't. Instead, they used the Ethical Zones that they themselves believed in. Why didn't they use another Ethical Zone? Remember, these zones are invisible to us. Second, it is hard not to be judgmental about others. It is easy to see others with different Ethical Zones as immoral as opposed to having a set of ethics that is different from yours.

Spiral Dynamics theory talks about the fear and disdain that people have for those in other zones. One of the things that I find most useful about Spiral Dynamics (which I haven't discussed much because it mostly overlaps with the other theories) is that it describes a new Ethical Zone, one in which people are aware of and appreciate the other Ethical Zones. Spiral Dynamics calls it the Turquoise Meme. I call this the Understanding Ethical Zone. As you read this book and work with the Ethical Frames model, you are moving into that Zone.

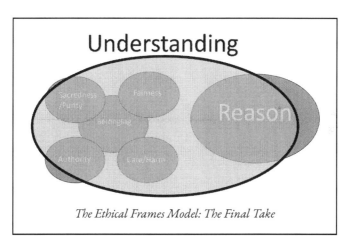

The Ethical Frames Model: The Final Take

Thus, even though Willer and Feinberg found that not many people can do this work (less than ten-percent), some people can. I think marketers and copywriters can be trained because they already have practice in taking into account other people's points of view. I'll go over the process of how to learn to reframe in the next chapter. You are about to move solidly into the next Ethical Zone, the Ethical Zone of Understanding.

CHAPTER 15
THE ROAD MAP TO A CEASE-FIRE: THE ETHICAL ZONE OF UNDERSTANDING

S INCE YOU ARE becoming one of the under ten-percent who could move into the Ethical Zone of Understanding, here's a road map I have created for how to get there. The steps include the following:

1. Recognize the importance that you place on the various zones by taking the quiz at https://www.yourmorals.org/
2. Understand both your and others' profiles by reading. Starting with this book is a good beginning, but if you want to go deeper, check into other resources such as *The Righteous Mind* by Jonathan Haidt and *Moral Tribes* by Joshua Greene, *A Brief History of Everything* by Ken Wilbur, and the podcast about Spiral Dynamics at http://www.theliturgists.com/podcast/2014/9/23/episode-5-spiral-dynamics.
3. Remember we are dealing with a paradox. Try to accept that you don't have all the answers, and that you can learn from others. That's called humility, which is a virtue. Spiral Dynamics warns that we may feel disdain or fear about the other views, but we need to not give in to that temptation. There may be something you can use in your life.

As ancient Chinese philosopher/poet Seng-Ts'an said:

Do not search for the truth; only cease to cherish opinions.
Do not hold to dualistic views, avoid such habits carefully.
If there is even a trace of right and wrong, the mind is lost in confusion.

4. Appreciate what the Ethical Zones that you don't place high importance on bring to our society and that you might be taking some things for granted.
5. Recognize that you also have those other Ethical Zones, even if they aren't as important to you. Identify them in your life or identify areas in which being aware of that Ethical Zone might be helpful. Work to increase your use of those other zones.
6. Here's a set of questions for you if you are Liberal and really high in the Care/Harm and Fairness Ethical Zones to be able to identify the ways the other zones may be at work in your life:

   a. Think about times when you felt cheated. Did that have anything to do with how much effort you put into it? (I bet it did!) That's the merit-flavor of the Fairness Ethical Zone.
   b. Did you ever do anything for a relative or friend that you wouldn't do for a stranger? (I am sure you did, including perhaps loaning money to a sibling or making a referral for a child or friend.) That's Belonging and Community.
   c. Who do you admire? Are you more likely to do something if they tell you that it is a good idea? That's Respect for Authority.
   d. Did you ever do something you disagreed with because your boss said to do it? Why did you do it? How did you feel afterward? Did you stay in that

job? That's Respect for Authority (or lack of it). If you lack it, what are the consequences?

    e. What's the one thing that you cherish most now or in the past? How would you feel if someone threw it out or destroyed it? That's Sacredness.

7. If you are socially Conservative, here are your questions:

    a. Think about someone you love. Perhaps your child or grandchild, or a spouse. Would someone from another country feel the same way about their child or grandchild or spouse? How would it differ? That's the difference that Belonging makes in the Care/Harm Ethical Zone.

    b. What would it be like to grow up knowing that you could never be equal to someone like you? What would it be like to face discrimination because of where you were born or what you looked like? That's what inequality feels like—a different interpretation of the Fairness Ethical Zone.

8. When you are in a situation with others who are not like you, listen to others using the vocabulary list. Try to determine what Ethical Zones they are drawing on when they say something.

9. Once you have been through these steps, you are ready to start developing alternative branding devices using the different Ethical Zones. The idea is to understand how closely each of the zones is associated with your product and how natural a fit they are. Pick an Ethical Zone that is active in your target group or try different ones.

10. Use the Ethical Frames vocabulary list to create messages. You can request the list at my website: www.ethicalframes.com.

11. Test the various emotional branding options among the target audience. You won't know if you got it right until you test it and see what effect it has. Some will fit better and have a greater effect.

a. Follow the steps in the measuring chapter. It's crucial to have homogeneous groups and to not confine yourself to major metros.

b. Use the image deck to elicit feedback that is more difficult for people to articulate.

c. Judge whether or not the effort is successful by the degree to which people pick up and use the words from that Ethical Zone in describing the effort.

12. You won't convince everyone, but look for a shift when you test it. If that didn't work, try again.

HOW REFRAMING MIGHT HELP

I'VE DONE A lot of work on how to reframe. I'll illustrate what could be done by using one of the examples I have been analyzing throughout this book: the Parkland shooting/Dick's Sporting Goods episode. Earlier, I concluded that violations of two Ethical Zones contributed to the negative reactions among Conservatives: Belonging and Community (being an American means owning a gun) and Sacredness (a gun has taken on a mythical importance). So Dick's (or anyone who wants to operate in this Ethical Zone) needs to know the qualities of these Zones. Dick's tried to use the Ethical Zone of Belonging (we support the Second Amendment; the CEO is a gun owner), but that wasn't enough. Here are some thoughts:

- Dick's could emotionally brand Dick's using its commitment to Belonging over time and that might work eventually. It could be as simple as consistently showing a lot of hunters in their ads. Because their commitment might not be believed (especially at first), consistency over time would help. Dick's appears to have decided against that for a rational reason (they are a low-margin business). Because hunters do buy other items, and, more importantly, the way hunters are portrayed might affect how others perceive Dick's, Dick's should reconsider their pivot away from hunters in order to emotionally brand to Conservatives using Belonging.

- Dick's should recognize that gun owners (probably) regard guns and gun ownership as Sacred. This should infuse everything they do, how they show guns, and the language of the way they talk about them. While the list of words for the Sacredness Ethical Zone might be too extreme, Dick's should test how to touch this area. Perhaps that work could center around the Second Amendment, demonstrating how Sacred that is to Dick's.
- The third Ethical Zone that is strong among Conservatives is Respect for Authority. Because the NRA has come out against Dick's, and because President Trump has not come out in favor of gun-control, they have two strikes against them. That means this approach won't work.
- What definitely won't work is an emphasis on one of the Liberal Ethical Zones, Care/Harm. Conservatives know that Liberals feel this way, so it is a tip-off that Dick's isn't talking to them if there is a focus on the Care/Harm Ethical Zone.
- My most controversial suggestion is that Dick's could be more aggressive in using the Fairness Ethical Zone. Fairness is more often a Liberal Ethical Zone, but Conservatives do care about it, just in a different way than Liberals—the merit-based flavor. By using a merit-flavored Fairness Ethical Zone, Dick's might be able to emotionally brand in a way that Conservatives would relate to. There are a few possibilities:

  - They could test a message that Dick's is trying to preserve the rights of gun owners by restricting gun sales to people who endanger that right.
  - Or it could try a message that the right to own guns needs to be earned by responsible gun use.
  - It could have a campaign that focuses on how responsible gun owners are, which has real gun owners (and Dick's customers) talking about how they appreciate that Dick's is taking a moderate stance.
  - The company could even create a nonprofit for Fair and responsible gun ownership and recruit

customers to join it. With the right language and concepts, that might turn the tide.

Creating options like these and testing them with the target audience is the only way to be sure these would work, but if you aren't familiar with the Ethical Frames of the target audience and you don't understand the emotional minefields that exist, then you can't create options. Even though Dick's understood that gun ownership was a hot button, they didn't understand the Ethical Zones, so they relied on the Second Amendment, and that they themselves were gun owners. That wasn't enough to counter the perception that Dick's wasn't on their side as indicated by Dick's gun-control lobbying efforts and destruction of the weapons. Reframing has been shown to work in other research; hopefully, it could work for Dick's.

ANOTHER REFRAMING EXAMPLE

THE LOWERED LEVELS of vaccinations of young children is leading to sporadic epidemics of preventable illnesses, such as measles. As I mentioned in the health chapter, the mothers who are antivaxxers appear to be both low in Respect for Authority and high in Sacredness. Thus, a campaign with a doctor won't work. What can be done? Here are some emotional branding ideas drawn from knowledge of the Ethical Zones:

- Since these mothers tend to be more often Liberal, the most successful campaign idea might be to use both the Care/Harm and Fairness Ethical Zones to talk about the disadvantaged children who have chronic illnesses who would die if they get the measles (the need-flavor of Fairness), and that vaccination of all children is the way to protect them.
- These mothers are high in Sacredness (even though they are Liberal), so a campaign about how disgusting the actual illnesses are could work. This could be indirect, by focusing on other illnesses such as the Spanish influenza epidemic. Remember, disgustingness is a powerful emotional motivator.
- Although these mothers are low in Respect for Authority overall so a campaign with doctors won't work, they do have

some people they hold in high regard. Finding mothers who fit that profile and highlighting that they decided to vaccinate their child (perhaps combining it one of the other messages) could be successful.

- Finally, although the levels of Belonging tend to be low among the Liberal women, a campaign that presented vaccination as the choice of socially responsible mothers (as Liberals would like to see themselves) might work, especially if combined with another message.

Again, no one *knows* if these particular emotional branding strategies would work, but it does provide some ideas for how the reframing technique can work for your brand.

CHAPTER 16
PLANNING FOR THE NEGOTIATION: DECIDING WHAT TO DO

THIS PATH ISN'T going to be easy, but it is possible. As you decide whether and how to apply the theories that this book has summarized, you may run into challenges.

First, you are also going to need to decide whether to conform to what are considered to be current best practices in marketing—tasks such as revitalizing brands by engaging younger consumers, using social media, and going premium. The emerging wisdom is that brands need to take a stand, and some brands such as Nike have demonstrated success.

There are problems with this approach. The Knowledge@Wharton blog notes how fickle young consumers are and even questions whether brand loyalty ever existed. I agree that you can't expect or plan for brand loyalty among young customers, and especially among Liberals, but contend that brand loyalty is alive and well among Conservatives. If your brand chases after Liberals, the loyal Conservatives will reject those brands.

The second issue is the profile of your consumers. What if your target audience is Conservative like Coors' was? Should you shrink your brand to become relevant? And even if your current base is Liberals, are you willing to sacrifice your full brand potential by alienating Conservatives?

You have an opportunity to go against the grain, to pick up market share among Conservatives. Or at least to not alienate them, by learning how to avoid the marketing landmines that have appeared due to political polarization. This is particularly important for those companies who have picked up the older brands that the major companies have jettisoned.

As you decide your route, be sure to use different assumptions in calculating ROI for the different directions. Use a much lower repeat rate for Liberals, because they will be chasing novelty, and a higher rate for Conservatives. How much different should the rate be? This needs to be researched.

Finally, there may be a conflict between your employees and your target audience. The most typical scenario is probably that your targets lean Conservative and your employees lean Liberal. If you have decided to go after Conservatives, you need to get your employees on board. You need to develop a way to deal with the conflict. You need to work with them so that they start to move into the Ethical Zone of Understanding.

CHAPTER 17

THE RULES OF
ENGAGEMENT: ETHICS

MARKETERS ARE UNETHICAL, the most unethical of all business people – at least according many people I have encountered outside of the business world. Those views aren't unique, research validates that many others agree. Marketers are viewed as puppeteers who manipulate poor uninformed consumers. Is this deserved? Sometimes yes, sometimes no. Regardless of its truth, while I was in seminary, I was a target for lots of anger from Liberals about unethical marketing practices.

These attacks opened me up to the possibility that marketers would use the knowledge in this book to manipulate customers. I decided that I would only feel comfortable writing this book if I included a chapter about marketing ethics, in general, and especially of emotional branding using the Ethical Frames model. And here it is, a chapter on ethics by a former practioner.

The minimum standard for ethics in marketing is whether or not something is true. Violating this can get you in trouble with the Federal Trade Commission in the US. In my religious world, this is integrity. Having integrity implies that one is honest and consistent in all aspects of their life.

That's a lot, but just telling the truth is not enough to be ethical; it is also important to not manipulate people. I love George Akerlof and Robert Shiller's definition of manipulation as when a marketer does something that will benefit the marketer but that is against the customer's best interest. Beyond the ethics, Akerlof and Shiller believe this practice leads to poorer economic outcomes. (Of course, they do, they are economists!) They are particularly concerned about behavioral economics principles that can hurt the consumer and the economy.

Akerloff and Shiller are responding to Cass Sunstein and Richard Thaler's book *Nudge*, which is based on the premise that people don't always make choices that are in their own best interest. A major focus of the book concerns the short-term decisions that people make which have negative long-term consequences. While nudging has been called paternalistic, Thaler defends his work by saying we need to always take into account human foibles.

To me, this implies a responsibility that the advertiser has for their customer. As we have learned from our deep dive into the Ethical Zones, brands have an Authority. To fulfill that role, they need to take responsibility for their customer. And because humans have a hard time with long-term time horizons, advertisers have a responsibility to think about the long-term customer needs. This means not starting something that they can't finish or continue with. Brands need to have a long-term vision, even if (or especially because) customers can't.

More than that, it is important for advertisers to respect their target audience. When advertisers look down on them, when they preach, they aren't being respectful, and they kill the connection the brand has with their audience. As we have seen throughout the book, brands are starting to take stands on social issues, but they need to be careful to take them in such as way that they aren't condescending and aren't preaching. Preaching only works with the choir. Respect your audience, even if you don't agree with them. That's both good ethics and good business.

In addition to the charge of manipulation, I heard other criticisms that I lump into two categories: bad marketing and marketing that isn't directed at the person criticizing it. People are outraged when marketing doesn't consider their needs and wants; that's bad marketing. Much of the time this type of advertising is done by a nonprofessional or marketing is being confused with selling. That's obviously not you, because you are reading this book.

The other category, marketing to people who have needs that the person complaining can't understand, is going to happen more and more in this polarized society. What you can do to deal with this is to improve your targeting and media buy so that nontargets aren't as annoyed by ads that aren't for them. The ability to target more and more finely is easier and easier with the internet and social media, so this should be relatively easy. However, even if you do that, you should also explicitly consider how those who aren't in your target group will perceive your ad. We often ignore them and then get blindsided.

Besides these two categories, other elements that I believe are unethical have to do with increasing bad outcomes in society. Shiller and Akerlof were concerned about bad economic outcomes but my concern is broader. This book arose out of the increased political polarization in our world. Anything that we marketers do to increase political polarization is unethical. This includes feeding feelings of fear and anxiety and reinforcing and/or increasing the belief that one group is better than another. Using fear can backfire as well. While fear can be motivating for your brand and work short-term, it plays on people's anxieties and may negatively affect their overall well-being. On a societal level, using fear and other negative emotions can create more divisions in society. Please don't do that.

As I discussed in the chapter on the Ethical Zone of Sacredness, disgust is another powerful negative motivator that can be combined with fear. Again, use it carefully and only when it is warranted and *never* use it to create bad feelings toward other people.

Another implication of this line of thought is that when people's needs aren't being met at a level, they regress. Thus, use of fear, disgust, and other negative emotions runs counter to the best interest of people being at their best. I claim that fear and negative-based advertising being used against other people is unethical because it can help to lead to an overall sense of people not doing well and to less rationality being used.

One marketer, who has made strides, created a code of ethics that is easy to understand. Citigroup hired an ethical advisor who helped them create this three-pronged standard that they use to evaluate the ethics of their actions:

1. Is it in our client's interests?
2. Does it create economic value?
3. Is it systematically responsible?

These questions are good for everyone to consider.

Thus, my code of ethics for marketing would read as follows:

- Don't lie; be honest; have integrity.
- Don't do something that isn't in your customers' long-term best interest.
- Precise targeting is good ethical behavior but consider how those who aren't in your target will react if they do see it.
- Don't do anything that leads to increased fear or polarization or leads to poorer outcomes systemically.
- Use fear and disgust responsibly.
- Be respectful.

Implementing the recommendation to only do things that are in your customers' long-term best interest can be difficult. It may not seem like the best course of action for the company, because it may sacrifice short-term profitability. We humans (even us marketers and advertisers—not just our target audience) are also subject to motivated reasoning. We convince ourselves that what we are doing is the best without truly examining it. We don't recognize it when we do it! So, we need a mechanism to hold us to it, perhaps by creating a customer sounding board to advise us.

Because marketing is generally regarded as unethical, it is even more important to be responsible marketers!

CHAPTER 18
REVIEWING THE BATTLEFIELD

C AN BUSINESS BE neutral? Until now, businesses tried to be neutral and ignore politics. That is increasingly difficult. From Merck's CEO Ken Frazier's decision to resign from President Trump's Business Council in response to the president's comments on Charlottesville's white supremacist rally, to Dick's Sporting Goods deciding not to stock assault rifles, to Nike's Just Do It ad featuring Colin Kaepernick, businesses are now deciding to weigh in on issues that are related to politics. Brands are exhorted to become relevant to consumers. As Jonathan Haidt posted on Twitter:

Jonathan Haidt @JonHaidt

Political polarization is changing the landscape for brands. In marketing, as in elections, you can win by turning out your side, rather than by appealing to the mass-market middle. If Nike's move is successful, we can expect more politics in our shopping.

Whether it works out for those businesses will depend. As a *Financial Times* article on the controversy stated, Nike's stock dropped in reaction to the news. However, their customer base is young and ethnic, so it will probably play well with their customers. In fact, Nike's sales the following weekend rose, it seems their emotional branding is working. As the *FT* reported, Nike had been losing sales and relevance to Adidas, and this was one way to get it back.

Paying attention only to Nike skews our perspective. As we saw in the Authority Ethical Zone chapter, the backbone of many brands are Conservatives. Because they are low in Respect for Authority, Liberals crave novelty, so they aren't loyal. Long term, Liberals probably won't stick with Nike unless they continue to innovate; otherwise, they will go after the next new thing. Other brands like Coors need to continue to appeal to Conservatives to maintain their brand.

While I am sure that Nike realized that they would set off a marketing landmine, I don't think Pepsi thought they would get the reaction they did with their Kylie Jenner commercial. I am sure they thought they were accurately reflecting their Liberal customer base's concerns, but they managed to blow it. Pepsi offers an example of what happens to a brand that chases after the fickle Liberals. Besides being easy to offend, Liberals are not the core of steadfast brand users. They prefer to find the latest craze. Thus, Pepsi will probably always come in second to the Conservative-leaning Coke, because Conservatives crave the consistency that brands provide.

This book has given you an overview of how political polarization creates marketing landmines and creates opportunity for emotional branding. Becoming fluent in this theory will change how you can navigate consumer emotions and how you make decisions. Even if you make the same decision, you will be clearer on what is involved and what the consequences might be. You can use the power of the Ethical Zones to take your emotional branding to the next level and avoid any potential marketing landmines in your path.

I hope you can see how deep-seated these Ethical Zones are for people and why they are hard for us to see. They involve hormones and personality attributes and brain functioning. This is why lecturing doesn't work and, in fact, backfires. Some will feel that I am downplaying how unethical "those" people are and that they need to be told. They have been told and it doesn't work. Although preaching may make the people feel as if they are doing something, it doesn't change anything. It just triggers a backlash and contributes to even more polarization.

I am hopeful that raising awareness and competence about emotional branding and marketing landmines will change the conversation. I am hopeful if marketers learn how to navigate Ethical Zones, they will not trigger emotions except when they want to. I want to continue the conversation about these issues. Please see my blog posts at www.ethical-frames.com and send me an email with your thoughts.

Further, if we as a society become fluent in the other's language, if we move into the Understanding Ethical Zone, my hope is that we will learn to respect each other's views and honor them. Let's increase the number of people with the Ethical Zone of Understanding. This might be the biggest change of all.

If you like this book and want to learn more, please check out my latest thoughts at www.ethicalframes.com.

AFTERWORD

A S THIS BOOK went to press, another brand took a cultural stand which presents an opportunity to explore slightly different issues. Gillette, Proctor and Gamble's shaving brand, created a one-and-a-half-minute video which opens with audio about "toxic masculinity" and the #MeToo movement. The voiceover then raises the question of whether "boys will be boys" should still be the norm and asks, "Is this the best a man can get?"

They definitely detonated a marketing landmine. The response on the internet has been strident, with indignant men vowing never to buy Gillette products again, among a chorus of sentiments such as, "Spare us your sermons."

This controversy is reminiscent of the Bonobo's #EvolvetheDefinition campaign, which questioned the definition of masculinity (a key element of the Belonging Zone). The one million dislikes on YouTube probably came from Conservative men; the men who like it are probably Liberal.

I include this because the Gillette ad raises new questions. When is it ok to preach your values? Does it matter if your target audience doesn't share your values?

On the one hand, as I've mentioned, a brand has Authority, so perhaps it *should* preach. However, that Authority only extends to its group. Because Gillette has sided with Liberals, Conservatives won't listen, and in fact, the strategy may backfire. Being preached to doesn't work—unless you're already in the choir.

Being perceived as condescending is a key indicator that you're talking to people who are operating in a different Ethical Zone.

There were criticisms from the Liberal crowd as well. As seen for other issues, Gillette were accused of co-opting the #MeToo movement. As one Liberal commenter noted, "the Gillette ad is just a cash grab." That's a Liberal "crime". Another criticism focused on P&G's own track record of workplace sexual harassment, as well as child labor and discrimination against Muslim employees. Make sure your own house is squeaky clean, or else you may get blowback if you take a stand.

Gillette likely conceived of this campaign to counter the market share losses they have recently experienced. Unlike Bonobo's, which is a young man's clothing company, Gillette wants to sell razors to all men. My prediction: Gillette will lose share among Conservative men and gain share among young Liberal men (except the most Liberal). It will also gain share among women for razor purchases. Their near-term financial results will be determined by how many of each are in their user base. Check my blog at www.ethicalframes.com. I'll report on my predictions as soon as Proctor and Gamble releases data.

What else could Gillette have done? If they wanted to persuade—instead of preach—they could have used the Ethical Frames reframing technique. They could still have taken a stand on the issue but in a more persuasive way. They could have reframed the issue, mimicking of the Texas Department of Transportation. If, like the Texas DOT, they had made it an identity issue ("real Texans don't litter"), Gillette could have made treating women well an attribute of being a "real man." That would have made men proud to use Gillette razors and wouldn't have created ill will. It wouldn't have been condescending and would have created a real sense of connection.

If only they had read this book. Or attended a workshop.

ACKNOWLEDGMENTS

I WANT TO thank my friends, family members and former colleagues for their encouragement and feedback. Denis's and Chris's willingness to act as sounding boards is greatly appreciated! The help with graphics and statistics from Laura Hoesly was immensely useful.

I especially want to thank my Monday morning and Saturday morning support groups and my Quaker Meeting in Plainfield, New Jersey, where I experienced the positive value of Belonging, Community, and Leadership. All of them have been instrumental in helping me grow as a person and becoming closer to the person that God wants me to be.

I also want to specifically thank the faculty of the Earlham School of Religion, especially Steve Angell and Lonnie Valentine, who among many others, encouraged me to develop my voice.

I also deeply appreciate the people who gave of their time and expertise by reading drafts of this book and providing me valuable feedback: Mark Ross, Anne Camille Talley, Chuck Merkel, Arlene Johnson, Bill Harvey, and Dick Vanderveer. Also, thanks to those who helped me shape an earlier presentation: Dan Reilly, Claudia Kienzle, Andy Kienzle, Krystal Odell, John Odell, Chris Cleary and Laura Hoesly.

My copy editor, Sandra Wendel, copywriter Kim Ledgerwood, and designer Elizabeth Gethering all provided skills that I don't have and value, thank you.

REFERENCES

Akerlof, George, and Robert Shiller. 2015. *Phishing for Phools: The Economics of Manipulation and Deception*. Princeton, NJ: Princeton University Press.

Amin, A. et al. 2017. *"Association of Moral Values with Vaccine Hesitancy."* Nature Human Behaviour 1 (12): 873-880.

Anderson, N. et al. 2017. *"Differentiating Emotional Processing and Attention in Psychopathy with Functional Neuroimaging."* Cogn Affect Behav Neurosci 17: 491-515.

Axt, Jordan. n.d. *Mapping Geographical Variation in Implicit Racial Attitudes*. Accessed November 5, 2018. https://implicit.harvard.edu/implicit/user/jaxt/blogposts/piblogpost005.html.

Babiak, Paul. 2006. *Snakes in Suits*. New York: Regan.

Bailis, Rochelle. 2017. *"Healthcare Innovations: CVS Rises in the Digital Pharmacy Age."* April 12. Accessed November 5, 2018. https://www.hitwise.com/articles/cvs-pharmacy/.

Birkner, Christine. 2016. *"Coca-Cola and Pepsi Are Both Losing Millennial Fans."* December 5. Accessed October 10, 2018. https://www.adweek.com/brand-marketing/coca-cola-and-pepsi-are-both-losing-millennial-fans-174956/.

BonzaiAphrodite. 2014. *"So Tom's of Maine Is Owned by Colgate. Let's Talk about It."* July 20. Accessed November 3, 2018. http://bonzaiaphrodite.com/2014/07/so-toms-of-maine-is-owned-by-colgate-lets-talk-about-it/.

Brown, Brené. 2017. *Braving the Wilderness*. New York: Random House.

Caspar, Emile, Axel Cleremans, and Patrick Haggard. 2018. *"Only Giving Orders? An Experimental Study of the Sense of Agency When Giving or Receiving Commands."* PLoS One 13(9).

Cho, Michelle. n.d. *"Benefit Corporations in the United States and Community Interest Companies in the United Kingdom: Does Social Enterprise Actually Work?"* Northwestern Journal of International Law & Business 37 (1).

Curtis, Valerie. 2013. *Don't Look, Don't Touch, Don't Eat. The Science behind Revulsion*. Chicago: University of Chicago.

Deaton, Angus. 2013. *The Great Escape: Health, Wealth, and the Origins of Inequality*. Princeton: Princeton University.

Dobin, Arthur. 2012. *"It's Not Fair! But What Is Fairness?"* May 11. Accessed November 3, 2018. https://www.psychologytoday.com/us/blog/am-i-right/201205/its-not-fair-what-is-fairness.

Edgecliffe-Johnson, Andrew. 2018. *"Nike Picks a Side in America's Culture Wars."* 9 7. Accessed 9 8, 2018. https://www.ft.com/content/c774408a-b275-11e8-8d14-6f049d06439c.

Edsall, Thomas B. 2012. *"Let the Nanotargeting Begin."* New York Times, April 15.

Friedman, Nancy. 2013. *"The Ads We Deserve."* June 25. Accessed 9 8, 2018. https://www.vocabulary.com/articles/candlepwr/the-ads-we-deserve/.

Gopnick, Alison. 2014. *"Even Children Get More Outraged at Us Versus Them."* Wall Street Journal, August 17.

Gopnik, Alison. 2013. *"Implicit Racial Bias in Children."* Alisongopnik.com. http://alisongopnik.com/Alison_Gopnik_WSJcolumns.htm#21Apr13.

Gopnik, Alison. 2013. *"How Early Do We Learn Racial Us Versus Them?"* Wall Street Journal, May 18: C2.

Greene, Joshua. 2013. *Moral Tribes: Emotion, Reason and the Gap between Us and Them.* New York: Penguin.

Greene, Joshua. 2014. *"The Cognitive Neuroscience of Moral Judgment and Decision-Making."* In *The Cognitive Neurosciences V*, edited by Gazzaniga. M. Cambridge: MIT Press.

Greenleaf, Robert. 1977. *Servant Leadership.* New York: Paulist Press.

Haidt, Jonathan. 2012. *The Righteous Mind.* New York: Vintage.

Hare, Robert. 1993. *Without Conscience: The Disturbing World of Psychopaths among Us.* New York: Penguin.

Hari, Johann. 2018. *Lost Connections.* New York: Bloomsbury.

Hetherington, Marc, and Jonathan Weiler. 2018. *Prius or Pickup?* Boston: Houghton Mifflin Harcourt.

Hibbing, John R., Hevin B. Smith, and John A. Alford. 2014. *Predisposed.* New York and London: Routledge.

Horgan, Terry, and Mark Timmons. 2007. *"Morphological Rationalism and the Psychology of Moral Judgment."* Ethical Theory and Moral Practice 10: 279-295.

Kang, Ha Young. 2017. *"Customer's Social Value Perception and Enterprise's Sustainability: Focus on Social Enterprise."* Journal of Marketing Thought 4 (2): 71-77.

Kangeisser, Patricia, and Felix Warneken. 2012. *"Young Children Consider Merit when Sharing Resources."* PLoS One 7(8).

Keane, M. et al. 2005. *"Confidence in Vaccination."* Vaccine 23 (19): 2486-93 .

Kington, Tom. 2018. *"Italy's Government Attacks Benetton Family over Genoa Bridge Collapse."* August 16. Accessed November 3, 2018. https://www.thetimes.co.uk/article/italy-s-government-attacks-benetton-family-over-genoa-bridge-collapse-p3wnkkrv0.

Knowles, Eric, and Sarah DiMuccio. 2018. *"How Donald Trump Appeals to Men Secretly Insecure about Their Manhood."* *Washington Post.* Nov. 29. Accessed Dec. 9, 2018. https://www.washingtonpost.com/news/monkey-cage/wp/2018/11/29/how-donald-trump-appeals-to-men-secretly-insecure-about-their-manhood/?utm_term=.f071de8494b7.

Konnikova, Maria. 2016. *"How We Learn Fairness."* *New Yorker.* January 7. https://www.newyorker.com/science/maria-konnikova/how-we-learn-fairness.

Langreth, Robert, and Matthew Herper. 2006. *"Pill Pushers."* *Forbes.* April 26. Accessed November 15, 2018. https://www.forbes.com/forbes/2006/0508/094a.html#6835ee1522ed.

List, Christian, Robert Luskin, James Fishkin, and Ian McLean. 2013. *"Deliberation, Single-Peakedness, and the Possibility of Meaningful Democracy: Evidence from Deliberative Polls."* *The Journal of Politics* 75 (1): 80-95.

Markovitch, Noam, Liam Netzer, and Maya Tamir. 2016. *"Will You Touch a Dirty Diaper? Attitudes towards Disgust and Behavior."* *Cognition and Emotion* 30 (3): 592-602.

Mason, LIlliana. 2018. *Uncivil Agreement: How Politics Became Our Identity.* Chicago: University of Chicago.

McAuliffe, Katherine, Peter Blake, and Felix Warneken. 2017. *"Do Kids Have a Fundamental Sense of Fairness?"* *Scientific American.* August 23. https://blogs.scientificamerican.com/observations/do-kids-have-a-fundamental-sense-of-fairness/.

Miller, Christian. 2016. *"Assessing Two Competing Approaches to the Psychology of Moral Judgments."* *Philosophical Explorations* 19 (1): 28–47.

Mooney, Chris. 2012. *Republican Brain.* Hoboken: Wiley.

Morales, Angela at al. 2012. *"How Disgust Enhances the Effectiveness of Fear Appeals."* *Journal of Marketing Research V* XLIX: 383-393.

Mycoskie, Blake. 2016. *"How I Did It: The Founder of Tom's on Reimagining the Company's Vision."* *Harvard Business Review,* January-February: 41-44.

Payne, Dinah, and Milton Pressley. 2013. *"A Transcendant Code of Ethics for Marketing Professionals."* *International Journal of Law and Management* 55 (1): 55-73.

Perry, Gina. 2013. *Behind the Shock Machine: The Untold Story of the Notorious Milgram Psychology Experiments.* New York: New Press.

Pinker, Steven. 2011. *Better Angels of Our Nature: Why Violence Has Declined.* New York: Viking.

—. 2018. *Enlightenment Now.* New York: Viking.

Putnam, Robert. 2000. *Bowling Alone.* New York: Simon & Schuster.

Raglan, G. et al. 2014. *"Need to Know: The Need for Cognitive Closure Impacts the Clinical Practice of Obstetrician/Gynecologists."* BMC Medical Informatics and Decision Making 14:122.

Ritter, Ryan et al. 2016. *"Imagine No Religion: Heretical Disgust, Anger and the Symbolic Purity of Mind."* Cognition and Emotion 30 (4): 778-796.

Rozin, Paul, Haidt, Jonathan, and Clark McCauley. 2008. *"Disgust."* In *Handbook of Emotions, 3rd edition*, edited by Jeannette M. Haviland-Jones, Lisa Feldman Barrett Michael Lewis, 757-776. New York: The Guildford Press.

Sagonowsky, Eric. 2018. *"Allergan was blasted for its unusual Mohawk patent license, and now it's a total flop."* February 26. Accessed November 5, 2018. https://www.fiercepharma.com/legal/allergan-s-controversial-tribal-licensing-pact-falls-short-ptab-scrutiny.

Sapolsky, Robert M. 2017. *Behave: The Biology of Humans at Our Best and Worst.* New York: Penguin Press.

Sashkin, Marshall, and Molly G. Sashkin. 2013. *Leadership that Matters: The Critical Factors for Making a Difference in People's Lives and Organizational Success.* San Francisco: Berrett-Koehler.

Scheepers, Daan, and Belle Derks. 2016. *"Revisiting Social Identity Theory from a Neuroscience Perspective."* Current Opinion in Psychology 11: 74-78.

Scholz & Friends. 2009. *"The Other Side of America."* August 12. Accessed November 5, 2018. https://www.adsoftheworld.com/media/print/queer_the_other_side_of_america.

Schweizer, Peter. 2008. *Makers and Takers: Why Conservatives work harder, feel happier, have closer families, take fewer drugs, give more generously, value honesty more, are less materialistic and envious, whine less...and even hug their children more than liberals.* New York: Doubleday.

Schwitzgebel, Eric. 2015. *"Cheeseburger Ethics."* July 15. Accessed Oct. 22, 2018. https://aeon.co/essays/how-often-do-ethics-professors-call-their-mothers.

Shrimp, Terrence, and Elenora Stuart. 2004. *"The Role of Disgust as an Emotional Mediator of Advertising Effects."* Journal of Advertising 33 (1): 43-53.

Sinek, Simon. 2017. *Start with Why.* Accessed November 3, 2018. https://startwithwhy.com/.

Skitka, Linda, and Anthony Washburn. 2013. *"Are Conservatives from Mars and Liberals from Venus?"* Claremont.

Thaler, Richard, and Cass Sunstein. 2008. *Nudge.* New Haven: Yale University Press.

The Liturgists. 2014. *"Spiral Dynamics."* The Liturgists Podcast. September 23. http://www.theliturgists.com/podcast/2014/9/23/episode-5-spiral-dynamics.

Tibbals, Karen. 2018. *Reactions to Drug Prices.* Green Brook, NJ: Ethical Frames.

Tracy, Jessica L., Conor M. Steckler, and Gordon Heltzel. n.d. *"The Physiological Basis of Psychological Disgust and Moral Judgments."* University of British Columbia. Accessed Dec. 10, 2018. http://ubc-emotionlab.ca/wp-content/files_mf/tracystecklerheltzelinpressjpsp.pdf.

Waldemar, Christian. 2018. *"Does Social Media Cause Depression?"* Psych Central. https://psychcentral.com/blog/does-social-media-cause-depression/.

Wasserman, Emily. n.d. *"Lamisil Digger—Novartis."* Fierce Pharma. Accessed November 15, 2018. https://www.fiercepharma.com/special-report/lamisil-digger-novartis.

Wilbur, Ken. 2001. *A Brief History of Everything.* Boston: Shambala.

Willer, Robb, and Matthew Feinberg. 2015. *"From Gulf to Bridge: When Do Moral Arguments Facilitate Political Influence?"* Personality and Social Psychology Bulletin 1-17.

Yourmorals.org. 2016. *Moral Foundations.* Accessed November 3, 2018. https://moral-foundations.org/.

ABOUT THE AUTHOR

KAREN J. TIBBALS is a passionate and accomplished marketing strategist, who has worked on over twenty brands and launched two billion-dollar products. She has worked on major brands at multinational firms such as Novartis and Merck, and also provided strategic guidance to others while she was at Ogilvy and Mather and Ipsos.

She holds an MBA in marketing from Rutgers University and an MA in religion from Earlham School of Religion. Her recent research has focused on how people apply their beliefs to their business life, with a thesis entitled *The Theological Basis behind Quaker Businesses*. Her previous publications include the chapter on "Early Quakers and Just Debt" in the volume: *Quakers Business and Industry* and the chapter titled "The Quaker Employer Conference of 1918" in *Quakers, Business and Corporate Responsibility*, and contributions to two journal publications: Confidence in Vaccination and Patient Counseling Materials.

Among the numerous awards she has received are an Effie for Pebbles Cereal, an International Award of Excellence for Pharmaceutical Detail Aid for the Diovan launch, and the PMRG Circle of Excellence Award for work on health literacy.

Her speaking engagements include talks at conferences sponsored by PMRG and PMSA, the SRI DTC conference, and the Leadership Conference. For ten years, she cochaired the PMRG Promotion Research Seminar. She has taught marketing and marketing research at Earlham College using the principles of experiential learning and has conducted numerous workshops for clients.

To contact her about speaking or workshops, see her website at www.ethicalframes.com.

45457434R00085

Made in the USA
Middletown, DE
19 May 2019